# Asian / Other

ALSO BY VIDYAN RAVINTHIRAN

POETRY

*Avidya* (2025)

*The Million-Petalled Flower of Being Here* (2019)

*Grun-tu-molani* (2014)

CRITICISM

*Spontaneity and Form in Modern Prose* (2023)

*Worlds Woven Together: Essays in Poetry and Poetics* (2022)

*Elizabeth Bishop's Prosaic* (2015)

EDITED

*Out of Sri Lanka: Tamil, Sinhala and English Poetry from Sri Lanka and Its Diaspora* (2023, with Shash Trevett and Seni Seneviratne)

*Angular Desire: Selected Poems and Prose by Srinivas Rayaprol* (2020, with Graziano Krätli)

*Arvind Krishna Mehrotra: Selected Poems and Translations* (2019)

# Asian / Other

## Life, Poems, and the Problem of Memoir

VIDYAN RAVINTHIRAN

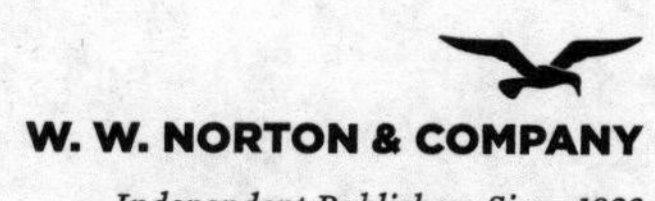

W. W. NORTON & COMPANY
*Independent Publishers Since 1923*

*Asian/Other* is a work of nonfiction.
Some names have been changed, along with
potentially identifying characteristics.


Printed in the United States of America
First Edition



Manufacturing by Lakeside Book Company
Book design by Brooke Koven
Production manager: Louise Mattarelliano

ISBN 978-1-324-02132-2

W. W. Norton & Company, Inc.,
500 Fifth Avenue, New York, NY 10110
www.wwnorton.com

W. W. Norton & Company Ltd.,
15 Carlisle Street, London W1D 3BS

10 9 8 7 6 5 4 3 2 1

Four months in North America. White graduate classmates are puzzled that a twentieth-century South Asian might share the experiences of a Medieval Jew. Their imagination stops at my brown skin. There has always been a civil war beyond the Northern Province. Those at risk cannot afford ignorance. I have learnt to recognize the languages of domination and gather a community of resistance for a dangerous journey toward necessary transformations.

—*Yasmin V. Tambiah*

The chameleon darkens in the shade of him who bends over it to ascertain its colours.

—*S. T. Coleridge*

# CONTENTS

# Asian / Other

# *Opening*

The fading light trembles like something alive—shy, shifting—on the wall abutting my childhood bed. I hear my son crashing down the stairs, and sounds of delight from my parents, for whom he can do no wrong. This is the room in which I grew up, in Leeds, in the north of England; the very wall to which I turned my head, rejecting conversation with family and refusing for years to attend school—studying at home, instead, alone, and achieving, like the precocious brown child I have never ceased to be, the grades required to flee to Oxford and reinvent myself.

It is the room to which, irrationally—how easy it is, to be retrospectively self-deprecating—I feared I'd never return, during the pandemic years when my wife, son, and I were isolated in the US (we'd only just moved there) by the travel ban. Unable to visit our families here in England or have them fly over to help us parent: What if my mother and father die, I used to wonder, before this is over?

The walls were repainted in bright colors by my father during my teenage years, to cheer me up. The sky-blue paint is giving way, its craquelure revealing the pink underneath—where that blur of sunlight expands and contracts like a single-celled creature only just now beginning to experience in the most minimal way what it is to be alive.

Visiting for Christmas, and with my parents helping with childcare, I am here to, by finishing this book, make sense of my past. Yet what life is, and how to live it—how, rather, it lives us—has never puzzled me more. The large subjects that I and my reader have in common begin to morph beyond understanding. What happens to identity politics, when we recognize that "identity" is nothing like as simple as we claim, and that we are often other, potentially mysterious, even to ourselves? What political alternative exists, to our incandescent, algorithmically envenomed appropriation—yes, I'm redefining that term—of world events to our dopamine-canalized, outrage-addicted brain chemistries?

"If you're not angry, you're not paying attention." How well does this stand up, to fury's commercialization? I speak of ragebait, forms of authorized egoism, and how rhetorics of pride may not cure subjugation, but exist in dangerous oscillation with it; also, of how powerful terms are trivialized (consumers "identifying" with pizza brands finding their own "voice"). Memoir is guilty too, when our styles of nonfiction, the stories we tell about ourselves, exaggerate the coherence and continuity of our personalities. Everyone becomes the hero of their own story, with others reduced to bit players.

I am reminded, by the engineered likeability of much nonfiction—where blurts of self-exposure seem to purchase the authority, to make generalizations—of the habit

South Asians have, of leaping to accommodate themselves to whiteness, by abbreviating and Westernizing their polysyllabic names.

—

ON THE LAST EVENING of my Christmas stay, with my son Frank safely asleep, and my wife at a restaurant with a friend, my parents offer to cook their famous spicy roast chicken—a Sri Lankan–British fusion unique to our household. The ingredients need to be inauthentic, prefabricated: Paxo stuffing, Aunt Bessie's roast potatoes, Yorkshire puddings sold by the frozen dozen. Then my mother applies her marvelous spice rub, and all is transformed.

As we're sitting down to eat, my father finds something to say. Clearing his throat, he asks—why is it that my four-year-old son, his grandson, doesn't yet know how to read?

Don't we know that reading is the portal to knowledge; that there is a reason schools for the gifted exist, in the US; is it not the case that Frank's peers are already ahead of him, that his teachers are shortchanging him, that we—my wife and I—simply aren't pushing him enough?

If you want the recipe for my mother's roast chicken—the rub that embrowns and textures those crappy potatoes and stuffing balls too, transforming even Bisto gravy into a luscious lava of colliding taste-sensations—you'll require one tablespoon of chili powder (the hottest you can find), half as much coriander powder, and quarter tablespoons of pepper, Jeera powder, and garam masala. Dry roast the mixture until aromatic. Stuff the chicken with as many unpeeled garlic cloves as it will accommodate.

For the argument about my insufficiently hothoused son, one can also list ingredients: substances explosive in isolation and, when combined, cyclonic. Not just immigrant ambition, or South Asian immigrant ambition, but the traumatized hyperurgency of Sri Lankan Tamils, desperate to elevate their children above and beyond even the faintest memory of harm (arson, rape, detainment, murder) "back home." Even to the holding camps Tamil children took their textbooks, to keep studying—learning English and becoming part of the colonial administration prior to Independence, was both how Tamils thrived and what brought upon them the retributive fury of the Sinhala-Buddhist majority.

"You taught yourself to read by the age of three! Give me one month with Frank, and he will know how to."

If, reader, you are a South Asian parent looking to get your child into Oxford or Harvard, and raiding these pages for advice: this is not the book for you.

—

CAN THERE BE EXCELLENCE without neurosis? Might the potentials within a child unfold spontaneously, organically, with guidance and encouragement, certainly, but sans shame?

This book is about how literature, and poetry in particular, provided me with a way out and a way in: with a place where the powers fomented in me (and I'll always be grateful for that) could unfold in unworldly, surprising ways.

"If poetry comes not as naturally as the leaves to a tree it had better not come at all," wrote the Romantic poet

John Keats. Forcing your child's growth, you might produce a prodigy. Or someone who'll never feel good enough, someone who lacks even in their most applauded and passionate pursuits that special bonus energy available only to those who've found—playfully and passionately—a path all their own.

—

FOR MANY SOUTH ASIANS a tension persists, between the identities we perform in the West, and forlorn or flourishing connections to the homelands our families either left behind, or exist in concurrently, with technology's aid: plane flights, phones with multiple SIM cards, video calls across the ocean. Making it possible, for instance, for my cousin in Sydney to not only speak with but also seem to *exist alongside* (he claims it's as good as being together) his father, who moved decades ago to Colombo after being imprisoned and fleeing his home in Trincomalee.

Imagine the scene. You're talking to an acquaintance, not an outright stranger or friend, and the conversation takes a turn. The light in their eyes dwindles and your colleague, peer, ally, glances to one side and begins to imagine a future beyond this conversation with you. Or, to something they've said you can't readily respond. You feel abandoned, cast out, an outsider. You have become, to quote the Romantic poet Samuel Taylor Coleridge, "a jarring and a dissonant thing."

How to grope toward that other state of being, in which—returning to Coleridge—"no sound is dissonant that tells of life"; where experiences of alienation can be lived through humanely and grasped as the impetus for structural change?

—

I ENVY, EVEN DISBELIEVE, writers with perfect, pungent, memories of their childhood. Mine's a blur. Once, I sat in a bashed yellow pedal car, for which my father constructed a roof-frame out of fiberglass rods. Craning over the steering wheel, I gazed at my mother—who stood in the kitchen of our first house in Leeds (a different one; my parents were warned off places in Yorkshire where their brown faces were *not* welcome). But I'm only remembering a photograph in an album. The memory is false. I am its spectator, not its subject.

My memories have been replaced by my mother's stories; reality has been displaced, by the myth she and my father, as Tamil immigrants to Yorkshire in the seventies, created around their high-achieving son. My parents decided I was a genius, when I was only a strange child: even hyperlexic children, as they're called, can't really *teach themselves* to read, unless you accept Plato's theory of anamnesis. She claims I never had a temper tantrum—except when craving a picture book about cars, that she didn't purchase until I sulked (and then she did), and which, over the coming months, I read till the pages tattered. In one of the tales in Hindu folklore of the blue boy-god Krishna, his mother Yashoda catches him eating dirt and pries his mouth open. Inside, chewed earth transforms as she watches into a working model of the universe. Stars, planets, everything, down to—I like to imagine—a recreation of Yashoda herself, peering into her son's mouth. "I should have bought that book at once," my mother cries—retelling the story to strangers. The message is clear.

I was a divine child; a gift; she should have listened to me, or rather to the force of unkillable Tamil brilliance uttering itself through me.

I was eighteen when I tried to kill myself. In love with a woman (twice my age and with two children) whom I'd met online, I now refused, having played truant for years, even to attend university—as my parents wished—here in England. My mother rejected a transfer to the US. Lying on this very bed, tracing my hand over the wall's ridged, sky-blue paint, I swallowed my father's heart medication. In the waiting room at the hospital, a friend asked my mother why she was there. She lied and said I had a fever—adding, after a pause, that I'd won a place at Oxford.

—

IMMIGRANTS OFTEN PRESSURE their children to excel. Those calcined by extremity, like Sri Lankan Tamils—a diaspora scattered by genocidal civil war—turn the screw with gusto. The child raised overseas must redeem the extended sufferings of their extended family, justifying generations of striving. But (here's the rub) it isn't asked only that the child high-achieve, but that they be *happy* about it. They must be continually, surpassingly, grateful on behalf of those who hadn't such opportunities.

"Minority" has changed meaning. One can now be of a large group (cis-het white women, for instance) and be designated, in terms of power rather than numbers, a minority. I return to the original definition, to speak for the *hyperminoritized*: those who exist as a minority (Sri Lankan Tamil) within a minority (Sri Lankan) within a minority (South

Asian). I feel for anyone who rarely sees on television a face resembling theirs; who gets left out of diversity initiatives in popular culture and working life; who doesn't feel spoken for, or represented, and may even doubt the assumption that representation *is* reparation; the sort who glimpses themselves in the mirror and is startled by their own sheer untelegenic weirdness.

For the hyperminoritized, connections have to be made, creatively and riskily, across dividing lines. To feel, sometimes, completely alone—is to drift toward a cosmopolitanism of unexpected, life-giving, overlaps between the experiences, the writing (the poems!), of far-flung people. I can't tell my own story (insofar as such a thing exists) without talking about poetry and the encounters with otherness it has made possible. And so I begin with South Asian poets, then proceed to people who resemble me less, or not at all. I hope that in this book, poems function as real, contestatory presences.

I'm not Indian or Pakistani or Bangladeshi or even part of Sri Lanka's Sinhala-Buddhist majority. I am a South Asian with little in common with other South Asians, let alone vast bureaucratic categories ("Black, Asian, and Minority Ethnic" or BAME, in the UK, the "Asian American and Pacific Islander community" in the US). Moving from England to the US, I have shifted from being a member of a politicized underclass with a civil rights history, attacked in the street, stopped and searched, passed over for jobs, mocked for our voices and features, targeted with hate-stares and slurs—to being part of a supposedly "model" minority whose sufferings, including white-supremacist murder, are rarely discussed.

—

HERE IS A SERIOUS DIFFERENCE between the UK and the US. Every British person of color I've met scorns BAME as a category. It flattens particularities: we use the term when necessary, but in, often, a bitterly jesting way. Is it a peculiarly British gift, to participate in conventions *ironically*? Certainly, for Americans, it seems that wholehearted acceptance, or to use the hideous phrase, "buy-in," is unavoidable. And so the manufactured demographic that goes by AAPI (or AANHPI, including Native Hawaiians) receives little pushback from progressives.

The problem is that "communities" cannot be stipulated into being. They form organically, as Divya Victor observes in her astringent, kinetic, multifaceted poetry (analyzing the murder of South-Asian Americans) on the subject of "kith"—as in, "kith and kin." "Kin" means those like us, who wear our names and faces, people we love as we love ourselves. "Kith" is something else; it is

> neither your mother nor your father nor your sister nor your brother; neither your grandmother nor your grandfather nor your aunt by blood nor your uncle by blood; neither your child nor your grandchild nor your great grandparent nor your great grandchild; neither of this generation nor the next nor the one prior; neither your cousin by blood nor your cousin by bone; neither inheriting nose nor skin nor brow nor boat; neither bestowing flesh nor tooth nor hair nor gait; neither in a manner of laughing nor holding a plate; neither descended from nor

ascending to; neither named for nor named after; neither of brood nor blood nor stock nor pool; neither possessing by claim nor disowned by name; neither baptized at the ancestral font nor buried in the shared grave; neither living nor dead nor born nor bred; neither passed on nor passing away; neither like nor unlike nor resembling tissue and cartilage; neither by birthright nor by death rites nor by divination nor miracle; neither by gene nor gestation; neither by womb nor tomb nor cuckold nor platoon *but* by what is sensed or seen or heard or felt in what moves between those not of blood and yet belonging together either on land or in air or in water or on paper; either through name or race or face or place of birth or blame; either as sign or shibboleth or overheard epithet; either as mark on a forehead or caught in crosshairs; either for paycheck or paper or map or license or visa; either by the queue or queue or queen or quill; either by mandate or state or decree or fiat of fate; either in law or labor or abode or abhorred; either by hell or high water; either by tongue or trade or tendency to wander; either as a manner of walking into rooms or crossing the arms; either by headdress or footwear or part of hair; either by grain or meat or milk or holy book; as the days of the week or the names for the moon; as a manner of love or as a manner of hate; as a manner of leaning or standing erect; either by ritual or by roads taken; by the way something pleats or drapes or hangs or is latent; as a way you move or are at rest by passing or failing another's test; either as a way of knowing or being known; either by the way a "we" exists or does not when we are not home; either as targets or by

> treason; either as a question of resemblance or in answer to a name: *kith.*

Victor's phrasing is fiercely melodic, her syntax a riffing on rubrics immigrants must ceaselessly navigate—she writes elsewhere of filling out yet another governmental form on her mother's behalf. She assesses what Paul Gilroy has called—a counterforce to Freud's "narcissism of minor differences"—"the invaluable solidarity of the slightly different," providing an alternative to the rhetoric of "community."

—

IN BOTH THE UK AND THE US, the label "Asian" effects erasures, but of different kinds: in one place, it's assumed to refer to South Asians, and in the other, to people of East Asian heritage. What *is* transatlantically shared, then, is a failure to grasp within prevailing coordinates the shadings of our planet's biggest and most populous continent. "Asians" are an afterthought. They're reckoned with blurrily, if at all.

—

WE HAVE IN THE UK a curious situation, where, despite being the country's largest minority group, South Asians often go without popular representation (will there ever be a brown James Bond?). When we do appear, a North Indian stereotype predominates: bhangra and Bollywood. Light skin, not dark.

This needs stressing. Dark brown South Asians like me

are, with fewer exceptions than I could count on the fingers of one hand, *completely* unrepresented on the small and big screen—I'm including Hindi films in this.

For lighter South Asians, makeup, technology, and careful lighting combine to idealize a complexion no brown person has ever had—I say this as the son of a vitiligo sufferer, and the father of a biracial, golden child. An entirely illusory, airbrushed hue, reminding me of a line from Elizabeth Barrett Browning's long narrative poem, *Aurora Leigh*:

> She was not white nor brown,
> But could look either, like a mist that changed
> According to being shone on more or less.

The South Asian must shape-shift to discover their niche in a visual hierarchy designed by, and for, others. You can be simultaneously stigmatized as socially undesirable—*and* as a slimy social climber who never earned their place. Though many South Asians become doctors, the one profession you'd think no one could gainsay.

—

SINCE, IN THE US, "Asian" rarely means *South* Asian, what other options are there? "Indian" works for some, but that word also refers to the Native people who have reclaimed it. "Desi" is popular, but often excludes Sri Lankans.

This slipperiness of identity means that South Asians are attacked both for what they are and for what they are not. Growing up in the north of England, my skin was repeatedly compared to excrement, but worse was being called a "paki"—the slur applied to all South Asians in the UK, not only Pakistanis, and rife in footage of the 2024 riots. Many of us have also been called the *n*-word, though, only in the US have I, personally, experienced the variant with "sand" in front of it. Islamophobia was at the center of the UK riots, and is also relevant in the US, where—though I'm not Muslim—I was, as a brown bearded man, accused at airport immigration of being a terrorist.

Sikhs have been killed by gun-wielding maniacs who thought they were Muslims and thought that all Muslims were terrorists. Sureshbhai Patel, an Indian grandfather visiting his family in Alabama, was identified by a caller as a suspicious "thirty-something Black guy": the police, when he couldn't understand them, slammed him to the ground and left him paralyzed. Was this anti-Black violence, or anti–South Asian violence? (The case against the police officer in question foundered when ten non-Black male jurors voted to acquit; two Black female jurors voted to convict.) Networks of exploitation and intergenerational trauma do not respect national borders. American exceptionalism creeps into our progressivism: those lamenting what the States have become still consider themselves special for occupying the place where all the important, terrible stuff is happening. They rarely consider multicultures the world over confronting their own legacies of violence.

—

APPLYING FOR A JOB in the UK (or when you have a poem published in a magazine) you fill out what's called an Equal

Opportunities form. We also find these five categories on the national census. Asians divide as follows:

**Asian / Indian,** ***a reference to the South Asian nation of India and British Indians***
**Asian / Pakistani,** ***a reference to the South Asian nation of Pakistan and British Pakistanis***
**Asian / Bangladeshi,** ***a reference to the South Asian nation of Bangladesh and British Bangladeshis***
**Asian / Chinese,** ***a reference to the East Asian nation of China and British Chinese people***
**Asian / Other**

In the 1950 and 1970 US censuses, South Asians were designated "other"—with a brief period in between, of being considered "white"; racial categories, including today's, aren't immutable. In England, South Asians used to be "black": this is how the great Sri Lankan Tamil theorist and activist Ambalavaner Sivanandan described himself; the Southall Black Sisters, and the Organisation of Women of African and Asian Descent, have brought together women from Asian, African, and Caribbean backgrounds in feminist solidarity since the 1970s. In this respect, the Americanization of racial discourse erases Britain's own civil rights history. Bhanu Kapil's *The Vertical Interrogation of Strangers* documents a shared Afro-Asian experience:

> By the end of the summer, my mother is living in a one-room damp-walled walk-up in Hayes, Middlesex, where George Orwell once taught grammar school English, and where a thirteen-year-old skinhead . . . pours milk

> bottles of urine into the black—the Paki, the Bangladeshi, the Sri Lankan, the Ugandan, the Ethiopian, the Jamaican, and the Gudjrati—letter boxes.

Kapil slides, across an explanatory dash, from "black," to a word flung at me many times: that slur white people, after a drink or two, endeavor to deconstruct. "It's not really offensive, is it? It's just short for Pakistan." By swapping "paki" into a list of nationalities—where it does take the place of "Pakistani"—Kapil skewers such complacence. She reminds us of a time and a place where "black" meant something different. Specificities—"Hayes, Middlesex," Orwell's teaching history, the "thirteen-year-old skinhead"—make for a constellation of data-points, each flickering and fading at the point of disappearing from view.

—

SO HERE I AM: the Asian/Other, slipping between categories. Identitarianism, now a mainstay of the Left, caused only death and destruction for Sri Lankan Tamils. During the riots of July 1983, murderers grabbed men off the street and smelled their hair. By the odor of the oil in it, they knew, this one is Tamil, not Sinhalese. They put a tire around his waist and set it on fire. Then they set his business, his dwelling, on fire. Sometimes his wife and children were still inside.

If South Asians are almost invisible, this gaseousness can be reconceived as a possibility. To not know—to not have already decided, aggressively—where you belong and who you are, can be liberating. I write in praise of uncertainty, curiosity, and an openness to otherness harder to maintain than we pretend.

Almost fifty years ago, Victor Anant wrote the following, in "The Three Faces of an Indian":

> It is in the nature of British civilisation to cherish people like me, homeless orphans. We are looked upon as children of conflict, born in transit, to be pitied. It is assumed that we will eternally remain torn within ourselves but that we can be taught to recognise our duality: the dear octopus of dichotomy never surrenders its victims. For nearly seven years, ever since I came to England, I have lived smugly and comfortably on the borderline, battening on the profits that derive from playing the role of cultural schizophrenic.

Half a century later, we haven't got much further. Let's consider experiences of displacement—literal (geographic), psychological, aesthetic—that, troubling the borders of being, have the power to both, as John Berryman said of poetry, "terrify & comfort." Moments when it is possible to imagine different ways to live, and have conversations previously impossible.

I see poems as continuous with those moments.

—

SRI LANKAN TAMILS relate perfervidly to not only English people but also the English language. During the colonial period, Anglophone schools appeared in Tamil areas. As a result, Tamils became fluent and found roles in the British imperial-administrative system. I reiterate these details since it's impossible otherwise to understand my parents' decision to move to England in the seventies—many Tamils had to flee the civil war, but where to? They chose not to teach me or my sister their language, seeing it only as a vulnerability. To them, proximity to "Englishness" represented both protection from violence and a path to success and acceptance.

We were sent to speech classes to speak English without a stigmatizing accent. My sister asked for her National Health Service glasses in brown frames, believing they'd be invisible against her skin and she wouldn't be bullied. My confused parents bought me blue, not black, shoes for school, and I was sent home. My father stocked our small, tired house with classics, unread, in fake leather from Reader's Digest. English literature represented something ideal, sacred—my sister took up drama, and I began raiding those shelves day and night. It was a strange situation. I was doing something of which my parents approved: but since they worshipped only the *idea* of those books, I didn't have to match them, overtake them, as lovers of literature (a friend of mine, son of an English professor, rebelled by reading only hard-boiled crime). Literature—soon, above all else, poetry—was *my* thing, a pursuit to be praised for but also an ideal privacy: a cabinet of secrets to unlock.

Since my teens, I've read poetry more or less continuously. In every spare moment, I pick some up. This is so instinctive it may be neurotic: a coping mechanism that has morphed into a vocation. In short, books have been for me what smartphones are for others. I am tempted to say, with the Romanian poet Ana Blandiana, that the page, written or blank (expectant), is my real homeland. I love words and how they go, collisionally, together, and if at any point the here-and-there teleporting style of this book, with its by turns ecstatic and browned-off, quarrelsome, and exulting sentences, feels oppressive, I hope the reader will understand my trying to share that sheer linguistic excitement which has meant close to everything for me.

—But I was speaking of poems. Unlike prose, short lyrics can be read quickly. Don't worry about failing to understand. This isn't school, there's no test to pass. It's an adventure. In a world of language debased and manipulated, a poem is a reprieve. A tactical, guerrilla reclamation of your powers of attention. Poetry restores to you the texture and taste of time, reminding you that the music of words needn't further the powers that be:

BISWAMIT DWIBEDY, "OPEN"

Turning the light on
the blue bodied boy
does he know how
to resist each morning
2 summers we are
riddled seers of

a restless sail and his memory
just stops by your hand

reaching for the day's mysteries.

Now it was time to think of coffee.

or syllables one must contemplate

when he calls out
a question you mishear

that is not what they want

We don't call that noise but
kingdom opposed to other things

Biswamit Dwibedy writes experimentally; his aren't poems where a single voice emotes clearly. Born in India, he has lived in the US and France: his poems don't belong anywhere in particular. They haven't clear footholds or handholds or signposts.

But I catch two Hindu references in this poem. The blue boy is Krishna, already mentioned; the "syllables one must contemplate" recall the sacred syllable "Om," signifying the unsayable mystery of life. "Let there be light," said the Judeo-Christian god, and Krishna in this poem does wake up and turn the light on. Each morning he must relearn how to "resist"—having forgotten overnight how to hold the world at bay. Maybe he's just "blue" as in, depressed. He's feeling blue. How can we help?

"His memory / just stops by your hand / reaching for the day's mysteries." You're also waking up, blinking into the sunlight, wondering what to do today. How unpredictable every day is. No matter how much we ruminate, predict, strategize, there is always something in tomorrow slightly different from anything we could hypothesize today. A changed light, exceeding the imagination. This is what it means, for the boy to be "reaching for the day's mysteries": Dwibedy works a cunning reversal of the Romantic poet John Keats's famous description of "negative capability,"

> that is when man is capable of being in uncertainties,
> Mysteries, doubts, without any irritable reaching after
> fact & reason—

This isn't anti-scientific: Keats means only that we shouldn't rush to protect ourselves against complexity by papering the world over with false explanations. (Conspiracy theorists have no negative capability.) Dwibedy's Krishna, if that's who he is, does the opposite: he reaches not for explanation but for those very mysteries we find so challenging to tolerate.

Someone—this boy—calls out to you, but you "mishear." Why? Because of them, "they," an oppressive conglomeration. The people who "want" something from him and from you.

Yet "we" have our ways of resisting. We're tuned in, to what the great Russian poet—internally exiled by Stalin, for satirizing him—Osip Mandelstam named "the noise of time." Is that what Dwibedy means by noise? Noise is (sound) matter out of place, meaningless, the opposite of music; neuroscientists explain our mood swings by pointing to the random "noise" the brain perpetually generates.

You and I and the blue boy, we know deep down our lives are more than so much noise. We call it something else: a "kingdom" opposed to that which they, them—whoever they are—press on us every day.

A poem is a tiny kingdom you can step into, anytime, and return from—readier to hold your own, no matter what comes.

# *Because you were there*

At school I was bullied by a boy named, here, Tom—for the usual reasons, centering my overweight gracelessness and my habit of "reading the dictionary," the accusation aimed at all brainiacs (though in my case, as I'll explain, it was literally true). Our sports field was some distance from the school itself: we bused it there for rugby on Friday afternoons. One day a different boy, whom I'd never met before, took the seat behind me and whisper-chanted (like a mantra) words audible only to me.

Drafting this chapter, I tried transcribing what he said, within what James Joyce derisively called "perverted commas"—being aware that literary conventions deceive as much as they enlighten. The effect was wrong: comedic, falsely immediate, too exactly the memoir-tone I, like many of us, have grown addicted to (reading books like this one) but also doubt. For the restrictions necessary to its conventionalized performance of selfhood. Its insufficiently skeptical mythologizing of disconnected events. And its failure to really reckon with—turning to the philosopher L. A. Paul—

the fact that, "just as knowledge about the experience of one individual can be inaccessible to another individual, what you can know about yourself at one time can be inaccessible to you at another time."

So let me describe otherwise.

It was a dreamily vicious, repeated pileup of vowels and consonants out to sound *ethnic*. Within this singsong, "paki" reoccurred at rhythmic intervals. A susurrus poured like poison—with a strange intimacy; the boy's breath touched my skin—into my ear.

—

THIS WENT ON for the entire twenty- or thirty-minute drive to the field. I was determined to ignore it. I left the bus without looking back, and in the changing rooms bumped into Tom. He looked at me and asked, did you hear what that guy said?

I played dumb. I will never forget the look in Tom's, my former enemy's, eyes.

"It doesn't matter," he said gently. "Just forget about it." And he walked off.

—

IN *BLACK STAR*, her study of Britain's Asian youth movements, Anandi Ramamurthy quotes Shanaaz Ali—a member of the United Black Youth League, an organization formed in 1981 in West Yorkshire, where I grew up.

> One of the kids said to me, "Oh go back to the jungle," or something like that. And there was this teacher, and it was

> interesting, I don't remember any of the names of all the other teachers but I always remember him. On one level I was quite frightened of him 'cos he was always quite strict and red-faced, Mr Wilkinson, and I remember him, kind of making a really big issue of it. He stopped the class and he said that, "I'm not having any of that" . . . And I suppose that stuck with me because it was somebody standing up for me.

Tom wasn't standing up for me, exactly. Or was he? I remember him—his face, gestures—whereas my memory of the racist is gone. Maybe I never got a clear look?

The white person knows a hurled slur has extraordinary power. It can create an everlasting memory. It is in the racist's gift—comparable to the supposed power of the lyric poet—to immortalize moments disappearing, otherwise, like, to borrow a beautiful phrase from *Blade Runner*, where it is spoken by an imperiled minority, "tears in rain." Yet the aggressor's particularity—their own name, face, accent—is typically sacrificed during this process, it doesn't make the record. The power they've gained comes at a cost, for in the mind of their victim, the bully tends to lose their name, features, personality, to an identification with the world of whiteness itself. In this erasure the slur's power resides. I am not made to feel that one person dislikes me (fair enough) but that they've spoken on behalf of a *community*—that dread word, again—rejecting all that I am.

As if not an individual, but the world, whispered or yelled the slur, that, even before it was uttered, lurked in the shadows, hid itself (not entirely successfully) within the most innocuous, sunlit, appearances.

—

DURING MY FIRST year at Oxford, I was walking to the English Faculty Library, preferable to the Bodleian because of its ugliness, which I found less distracting. Weighed down with books, I carried over one shoulder the satchel which has semipermanently damaged my neck and back (all those tomes!) by causing—said a physio, years later—an asymmetrical development of the muscles. The sun shone coldly, rockets of purple buddleia overhung the path, and along the wall of the cemetery patches of bird-shit glowed like grain-mustard.

A car drove past (these incidents often, I've noticed, take the form of "drive-bys"):

—Go home, paki cunt!

—

THIS IS HOW JOYCE represents speech, forsaking those perverted commas for the dash used by French novelists. It seems right for what happened here, because of the speed, and how the words (and a chucked bottle) came at me before I could respond.

Let us scrutinize this assaultive phrase, cloven (a caesura, resembling that of Old English verse) by the (spoken, implied) comma. "Go" and "home" repeat a vowel sound: it's what scholars of poetry call assonance. "Paki" and "cunt" are consonantally linked by those guttural *k*'s. Except that sound preexists these words, it is in "go," kickstarting with its harshness the whole exclamation . . .

Growing up with a speech impediment, I learned to look hard at words for their quirks. Studying poetry, this trick, or tic, or compulsion, came with me. Deconstructing that slur meant taking control.

Suffice it to say, this event stands in for countless others—the injury, the immediate pain, the reflective response. I don't know if the person who yelled those words remembers: it seems unlikely.

—

I HAD WORD-SOUNDS on the brain, having been asked to write—the sort of essay you'd *only* get set at Oxbridge—on "acoustic texture in the poetry of Andrew Marvell."

Marvell wrote in a time of civil war. The tensions of that moment ruffle the patterns of his poetry. But poems don't have to be considered entirely in terms of where, and when, they were written. Marvell wrote "Music's Empire" in 1650. This was (his poem had no relation to these events, until now) the period of Dutch control of Sri Lanka, where a distinctive racial subculture, that of the Burghers, continued to evolve. I mention this because Marvell's poem approaches, more than music, the wider realm of *sound*—including the power of words—through imagery of empire and colonization. It begins:

I

First was the world as one great cymbal made,
Where jarring winds to infant Nature played.
All music was a solitary sound,
To hollow rocks and murm'ring fountains bound.

II

Jubal first made the wilder notes agree;
And Jubal tuned Music's first Jubilee:
He called the echoes from their sullen cell,
And built the organ's city where they dwell.

Nigel Smith explains how this poem varies the conventional comparison between music and "state-building," and music as corresponding to "heavenly harmony." In Marvell's poem, there's something more voracious, viral, about music. Bound, originally, to such sticks and stones as, we're told by the children's rhyme, may—unlike words—break our bones, music is freed from this confinement by Jubal, who in the Bible (Marvell's playing with his name) "tuned Music's first Jubilee."

Many of us now believe that words can and do cause harm. That speaking (or writing) and doing are not so far apart. Sometimes I agree. Sometimes I fear we have erased an important distinction, through needing to believe that the opinions we share, the words we write and read, have a direct and undeniable impact on the world.

*Go home, paki cunt.* Compare this to—I'd hear it often, aimed at gay people in Cincinnati in the early 2000s: *God created Adam and Eve, not Adam and Steve.* It's that rhyme. When sounds come together, a statement seems to be true. It becomes memorable: an earworm. It spreads. The secret of poetry degrades into hate speech.

Jubal *made* the notes agree, he called out the echoes from their "sullen cell."

"Go home, paki cunt."

---

AMBALAVANER SIVANANDAN—that Sri Lankan British Tamil theorist and activist—devised the pithiest response to "Go home." He wrote into the history of British racial justice seven words to cleave to. Not responding in the moment can be self-destructive: it means revisiting the assault in your mind, wishing you *had* said something. You agonize, wishing you could time-travel and tell that racist what's what. It's a trap: another way for racism to prevent you living your life.

When the racist says, "Go home," reply (actually or mentally): "We are here because you were there."

---

III

Each sought a consort in that lovely place
And virgin trebles wed the manly bass.
From whence the progeny of numbers new
Into harmonious colonies withdrew.

Marvell's scansion—his control of meter and rhythm—is impeccable. These skills were referred to as a poet's "numbers," because it meant counting syllables. But this stanza rumples, when we're told "the progeny of numbers new / Into harmonious colonies withdrew." The line about the colonies slows down, it is subtly *dis*harmonious.

"Numbers," here, means musical notes. But linked to "progeny," it also suggests the expanding population of "colonies" overseen in the Global South by—it's the title of the poem—"Music's *Empire.*" "Each sought a consort in that lovely place / And virgin trebles wed the manly bass": consider these lines alongside what was happening in Sri Lanka at the time, under Dutch control—as colonizers wed the colonized, and Burgher subcultures came into being. The gaze of empire depicted lands as virgin (i.e., unhistorical, inexperienced, untouched, as if no one lived there already; also, ready to be ravished, raped, conquered, taken into Western possession). The so-called natives were often, in these accounts, gendered as female, according to the sexist framing which associated women with irrationality and an inability or unwillingness to govern themselves. Like women, it seemed, dark-skinned people needed to be taken in hand—for their own good.

An act of power is being reframed as musical composition. One country takes over another, and this is pictured as the creation of harmony out of disharmony.

—

*We are here because you were there.*

Sivanandan's context is postwar immigration to the UK, the situation described by Ian Sanjay Patel:

> Between 1945 and 1973, Britain began a painful transition from world imperial power to postimperial power. Simultaneously, in these years it entered a period of domestic transition within its shores, moving from a relatively mono-ethnic and monocultural society towards a multicultural and multi-ethnic one.

> . . . By the end of the 1950s, non-white British and Commonwealth citizens now settled in Britain began to record the intricate hostilities they faced. . . . Susunage Weeraperuma, born in Ceylon, who arrived by ship in Southampton in 1960 . . . soon began studying law at Lincoln's Inn in London. Part of life as a non-white migrant to Britain was a daily rehearsal of slurs. As he wrote in the early 1960s: "Another glaring example of prejudice occurred when I accidentally trampled the foot of an elderly woman in a London street. My instantaneous apology was ignored and she screamed frantically, 'Coloured Indian bastard!' "

If only Weeraperuma had Sivanandan's words to hand. Or those of the Asian Youth Movement: "Come what may, we're here to stay!" This is street poetry. It is the music of language placed in the service of rebellion. "Police tey nah ithbar haro, apni raki aap karo"—Don't rely on the police, defend yourself!

*We are here because you were there.* The racist is reminded that dark-skinned people exist in this country, their country, because of what white people, their people, have done overseas. They—the colonizer—become the one who should have stayed at home.

Yet the Global North (including its people of color) is *still* sucking the Global South dry of resources, prospering by stealing its wealth. Aren't we talking about neocolonialism, when we consider Bangladeshi garment workers producing clothes for US and European fast-fashion labels (Beyoncé's Ivy Park clothes are made in Sri Lanka, in Negombo), or countless acts of climate destruction—

such as the damage done to the Ogoni people in Nigeria, by Shell Oil?

So maybe we shouldn't say, "We are here because you were there," but "We are here because you *are* there."

—

AND YET: the present-day racist is unhistorical. He sees no link between the past and present. Between empire and immigration. As such, he is unopen to the dialogue Sivanandan imagines.

—

ANOTHER TYPE OF COLONIZATION to consider—a figurative kind, but painful, and everyday, personal and political at once—is the colonization of our thoughts by those who've injured us. And how we, subsequently, mentally colonize our environments with our grievances: the pain of the past. As Ada Limón puts it, in "The Great Blue Heron of Dunbar Road":

> the valley
> when you first see it—the small roads back
> to your youth—is so painfully pretty at first,
> then, after a month of black coffee, it's just
> another place your bullish brain exists, bothered
> by itself and how hurtful human life can be.

This is an eco-poem about how we hurt our environment, but with two meanings. We go to nature to escape, yet saturate it with our own anxieties—our minds full of baggage we can't leave behind. The mental error, of filling the "valley" with our own concerns, prefigures the grosser error, of dynamiting or felling or drilling into or concreting over what should be left well alone.

Why is it that I'm so determined to imagine my way into that racist's mind? Why do I want so strongly to believe that it was a one-off, a drunken pisstake, nothing more—a lad being edgy for laughs?

The first time a racial slur was yelled at me (again from a car), when I was out with the woman who'd later become my wife, *I apologized* to her.

—

WE USED TO TALK about "living rent-free" in a positive sense: as in, when a song or meme turns up that we can't stop thinking about. But I've witnessed online a shift in meaning. Now, when you mention "living rent-free in somebody else's head," it is, apparently, an achievement: to have an opponent obsess over your clapback. The astonishing cost of housing for my generation and the next is surely relevant: lives are increasingly shaped, in the real world, by the impossibility of buying houses, and the necessity of renting at enormous cost.

The racist is living rent-free in my head. I should do something about this. I should snap out of these thoughts and rededicate myself to the present moment—to those I love, instead of, while playing with my toddler, drifting off into the past, while his (my son's) behavior subtly changes, he scampers to regain my attention, and in this microscopic yet momentous way, racism touches him too.

In this way, I begin to worry about worrying—resenting what is called white supremacy less than I resent myself, for being so haunted and porous.

But what I hate still more is the idea of living rent-free in *the racist's* head. I don't want to be important to him. I don't want a twisted version of myself trapped, like one of the digital recreations of a person's consciousness in Charlie Brooker's *Black Mirror*, inside his skull.

—

IV

Some to the lute, some to the viol went,
And others chose the cornet eloquent.
These practising the wind, and those the wire,
To sing men's triumphs, or in heavens choir.

"Some": Marvell's ambiguous phrasing has me read his poem against the grain, touching histories it was never meant to engage. Before, he spoke of "echoes," "numbers," the musical notes Jubal extracted from nature and built into a "city." By this point, "some" appears to refer to *people*, free to choose which instrument to play. We're told that empire hasn't enslaved others but set them free to express themselves.

Regardless of skin color, nationality, or other details of subject position, we are all the people we are, living the lives we live, because of an immense network of causes and effects connected to migration, war, the distribution of natural resources, and global trade. Uncountable impulses, decisions, acts of chance, victories, and defeats had to occur to bring you to this place, the moment in which you read this page. To inquire into one's DNA and discover connections to multiple continents and racial groups, is but the tip of the iceberg.

In this situation, the situation, I repeat, of *all of us*; the "world" in which, to quote William Wordsworth, "we find our happiness, or not at all"—the only, ecologically fragile, multifariously exploited, world we have—the lie of the entirely free-willed individual obscures our embeddedness in patterns of power elusive of our understanding. And often, when we get angry (this applies even to our activism, when it has no political result), we are merely being loud to pretend to others and to ourselves that we are self-determining. To assert a falsely solid sense of personhood—like much memoir.

Shouting "go home" at a brown person out the window of a car may produce a feeling of release, excitement, of freedom, from enchaining proprieties. It may feel like aliveness itself. It denies another, gloomier, more nebulous feeling: that you're disjointed, you don't know who you are; that your decisions are echoes, after-ripples, nothing more, of events beyond your control, happening decades or even centuries prior to your birth. To shout a slur is to make a noise, to hear yourself, even to—in a distorted sense—"sing men's triumphs."

—

I'LL APPLY THIS STANZA of Marvell's poem more directly, to the choices my parents made both in and out of Sri Lanka in response to British rule. Following the Napoleonic Wars, the British took over Sri Lanka (then Ceylon) at the beginning of the nineteenth century, and stayed in control until Independence in 1948. Tamils were demonized by the Sinhalese for rising above their station by cheating (one can draw parallels with Jewish people making the most of their constraints, moving into finance and being blamed for it). In turn, Tamils of my parents' generation conceived of English, and England, as a route out. This is why, when my parents emigrated, they moved to England; but could it also be why I am today not the doctor or engineer that South Asian children are stereotypically encouraged to become, but a professor of English literature?

"Some to the lute, some to the viol went, / And others chose the cornet eloquent." The immigrant turned stylist (prose writers fit the bill, as well as poets) has to wonder: Where does my eloquence come from, and what do I want to do with it? In what context was my father's decision made, to practice medicine in England rather than Sri Lanka? Only an apologist for empire could see these choices entirely in terms of liberation. Marvell's poem helps me understand how a person may seem but an "echo" within a continuum of historical noise. "Freedom is what you do with what has been done to you." At what point does the postcolonial person change from being a musical note, in a global symphony written and largely performed by others, to an individual with some power over their own future?

—

ANOTHER WAY OF PUTTING the question would be in reverse: How do many persons come together to make a society, while each remains free? Explaining that the end of Marvell's poem, mentioning a "gentler conqueror," refers to either his patron Fairfax, or Oliver Cromwell, who'd become—following civil war, in England, in the seventeenth century—"the consummate master musician of the protectorate state, knitting together the different parts of the political fabric," Smith spotlights the poem's central metaphor. This is where music becomes both an "empire" and a "mosaic":

V

Then Music, the mosaic of the air,
Did of all these a solemn noise prepare:
With which she gained the empire of the ear,
Including all between the earth and sphere.

VI

Victorious sounds! Yet here your homage do
Unto a gentler conqueror than you;
Who though he flies the music of his praise,
Would with you Heaven's hallelujahs raise.

A mosaic presents one picture, but in many parts. Lots of little pieces, like musical notes in the aforementioned symphony, come together to make something larger. Perhaps a mosaic contains within itself, and overcomes, the idea of explosion, rupture: they seem to *include* the possibility of their vanishing, and yet to outspeed that possibility, because the divisions between pieces are regular, and were part of a contained (often ancient, yet surviving) creative process.

One can read an idea of society, and of the atomized person, into these affecting arrangements of pixels of color.

As he previously leapt, associatively, in terms of sound, from "Jubal" to "jubilee," Marvell now leaps from "music" to "mosaic." This creates the impression that he is coming up with his metaphor in the very moment of writing the poem. It also fuses with colonial endeavor what feels like the *autonomy* of music, sound, as it is liberated from nature by man, and starts, like some kind of malevolent AI, to write its own story—creating an "empire of the ear," where sound determines, creates, meaning, not the other way round. It is as if, because "music" sounds like "mosaic," it must be a kind of mosaic.

My introduction discussed noise, and a poem as a kind of kingdom. Marvell and Biswamit Dwibedy come close, then, as one wouldn't expect of a seventeenth-century English metaphysical poet and a twenty-first-century experimenter. Marvell points to something about music, noise, "empire," and poetry itself, that, self-propelling, will always exceed our designs. In the final stanza, he requests of music that it forego its own "empire of the ear," and subordinate itself to Fairfax or Cromwell, a man wishing to build a better state, who doesn't want praise from others, but modestly to use his voice, his own song, his own music, to praise God.

—

*Go home, paki cunt.*

The racist shaped noise into spoken words, just as music is a shaping of noise into harmony: I understood him, the sonic shape he put across echoes within me, establishing, as with a musical motif, resonances with my life's other, at first seemingly unconnected, events.

What is an event, anyway? It is an attractively drawn chapter, of a memoir telling a tale of overcoming or at least transformation, of change achieved through suffering and, in response to suffering, resilience. Do I believe in such narratives; do I wish to construct one here; what pen or pencil has the magical power, of circumscribing the flow of life into events with set beginnings and ends and a place in the plot?

Writing, as Marvell suggests in his poem, is also about converting noise, which is shapeless and meaningless, into music: poetry, not prose, is where language comes closest to music, where it tries to communicate something, but in the knowledge that an overplus of sound exists, that may either frustrate that meaning, or affirm it, or—and this is most interesting to me—encode a different, second, a counter-meaning *hidden within and experienced through sound itself.*

The *o* sounds, the *k*'s, the vowels and the consonants: the English language belongs to both me and the racist, providing a means of expression (which also means: a conduit for violence), while existing, too, as an empire in itself. A realm of sound and meaning we may enjoy the illusion of contracting into a single thrust, a single yawp out the window of a car, or a line of a poem—but which is in fact uncontainable.

—

MAYBE MARVELL'S REALLY *pleading* with music, to come back under human control. To relinquish its independence. Music, in his poem, is like a colony (Ceylon, now Sri Lanka) seizing its own destiny, no longer requiring a foreign power to order its affairs. He tries to flatter this force, to persuade it, using the opposite of a slur—through, that is, "praise": "Victorious sounds!" He acknowledges the victory of music over human control, in trying to convince music to reverse that victory.

You come across a word in a poem that feels queasy, that doesn't sit right, and sometimes you can explain this, and sometimes not. "Victorious" is an ugly word to those of us not as interested in victory, or defeat (in, that is, power), as neo-Victorians are. What are the relational alternatives to victory or defeat—thinking both in terms of fraught encounters (a racist yelling at you out of a car) and more globally, politically (in terms of the British Empire, without which the person that I am would not exist)?

Having read this poem many times, I've come to feel that "victorious" both looks, and sounds, odd, because of its resonance with "harmonious" earlier on—that line about colonies manifesting in its rhythm the very disharmony, or excess (linked to population growth), it ostensibly disavows. "Harmonious" and "victorious" are adjectives painting the best, most flattering, picture of a situation. But their chewy feel in the mouth, the way they obtrude on the poem's meter, makes them stand out as word-choices made in a particular moment, replaceable by something else—these words don't sound *inevitable*. One way to win might be to convince one's opponent that they are already "victorious": to fool them. But as I've said, I'm more interested in alternatives to winning and losing, domination and subordination. It is because this poem's answers to the questions it asks are insufficient—

the questions outlast the answers, like the echo of an immortal music hanging in the air—that it continues to haunt me.

—

*Go*
*home*
*paki*
*cunt*

Thank you, Tom.

# *Start thinking and stop living*

As I was writing, something happened—startling—a spider, tinily scrambling, and with a white belly like a bead of milk, dropped down from the ceiling. It hangs, now, higher up, enclosed in itself, a tiny dark oval. I didn't know spiders did that with their legs, except when dead.

The spider arrived as suddenly as that slur, twenty years ago. Those words, like other excruciating memories, *re*arrive in my mind at the unlikeliest moments. My brain is faulty hardware. I don't know why, unlike a character undergoing an epiphany in a book or onscreen, it is impossible for me to transcend past injuries once and for all. Deep within, it seems nothing is ever satisfactorily, only tendentiously, resolved. My self-cures are provisional, they only function in certain lights.

Fear is curious to think about. I was once more frightened of spiders than now—than I was, when the spider descended. It appears that, just as I am capable of being unexpectedly weaker, more doubt-ridden, than previously—even a minute ago—there are also experiences ahead of me, when expected tremors won't materialize, but swap out for windows of clarity.

Some fears are archetypal, others cultural—with discussable wellsprings. I became scared of spiders since my sister, ten years older, hated them with a hatred going back to a childhood that in every other way she can't remember (including the Tamil she once spoke in Batticaloa). Her cousin collected spiders in a bucket and threw them at her. That was the beginning of the fear that, unlike a language, she could not forget—or unlearn—and which I inherited and have carried across the world. My phobia is nothing but an echo: a facile, displaced rhyme placed too far from its partner, so that, reading the poem of my life, you don't even hear it.

Now, in the US, and following the birth of my son, I find myself capable of taking spiders and dropping them outside (as my son Frank insists): this *non*-fear fascinates me. My sister ensured her sons wouldn't inherit her arachnophobia, by, whenever she saw one, probably the little money spiders we have in England, or a daddy longlegs, which isn't really a spider at all, having them play with it. I don't wish to pass onto Frank a cascade of anxieties; but why is it, in this case, relatively effortless? I don't need to try so hard (as when he climbs high at the playground, I must actually turn and walk away, leaving my wife to watch over him) to be unafraid on his behalf—about spiders. It's as if his coming into the world, and my becoming a father, and our moving from one country to another, the year after his birth—in January 2020, right before the pandemic—has changed my instincts. The brains of fathers, as well as mothers, alter when a child is born; or was it the act of migration—my taking up, and revision, of the journey my parents made, not from England to Massachusetts, but from Sri Lanka to Leeds—changing me, deep down in my bones?

The Northern Irish poet Tom Paulin—my tutor at Oxford, who set that crazy essay on Marvell's "acoustic texture"—translated a poem by Victor Hugo about spiders:

> Really because we hate them
> I try to love the spider and the nettle
> —the nettle has a hairy stem
> —no *hairy stalk* would be better
> and the spider has wire legs
> brisk and bent below a body
> like a tiny egg
> —nothing but nothing fulfils
> and everything punishes
> their mournful hope
> —they're damned dreggy meagre
> so one might as well
> love a piece of old rope
> —like grey underpants
> they carry the stain of the provincial
> and can find nobody
> to admire their vernacular
> they're wee victims
> of nature and history
> who bring a taste of some minor abyss
> bring grot and gloom
> —ack they're like shattered limbs
> or the shut smell of piss
> in a basement room

Influenced by Eastern European poetry, Paulin turns the spider into a torture-survivor, an abased minority. I think of Tamils bundled, during and after Sri Lanka's long civil war, into white vans—snatched off the street—and detained without trial; beaten, raped, having their teeth torn out with pliers and plastic bags pulled over their head with petrol inside, so they choked on the fumes; being compelled to sign false confessions, admitting collusion with terrorists.

Paulin's style includes afterthoughts, it designs itself as it goes, using unexpected rhymes as stepping-stones. Placing dashes at the beginning of his lines, he turns his poem into a speech act with so many exclamatory bursts: a voice that seems clumsily digressive nevertheless gets the job done, rather as a spider manages the movement of its eight legs across the floor. We should try to love the spider, says the poem, precisely because we are programmed, it would seem, to hate and fear its otherness, the uncanniness of those frittering "limbs," which seem (going back to mosaics) like something "shattered" already, something that shouldn't be alive, that is both excessive (*eight* legs!) and perversely disorganized. When you see one, the heart quops, and it's that moment—the "taste," of a sudden, "of some minor abyss"—on which the poem concentrates. The abruptness of seeing a spider out the corner of your eye, and flinching, matches the abruptness of the poem's last, devastated, flare-up: "ack they're like shattered limbs . . . "

—

HERE'S ANOTHER POEM about spiders, Nikki Giovanni's "Allowables":

I killed a spider
Not a murderous brown recluse
Nor even a black widow
And if the truth were told this
Was only a small
Sort of papery spider
Who should have run
When I picked up the book
But she didn't
And she scared me
And I smashed her
I don't think
I'm allowed
To kill something
Because I am
Frightened

Giovanni was central to the Black Arts movement and the Black Power movement, and while there is no reason a poet of color should be obligated to write about race, or assumed to be always writing about it, the colors "black" and "brown" are as important as the femaleness of the spider. "Recluse" and "widow" also leap out, to turn spiders into ostracized people. Racists consider Black and brown people "murderous"; women can be stereotyped as vengeful "black widows," but the killing of Black men by police also potentially makes for thousands of "black widows" in another sense. There's something literary about this spider. It is squashed by a book, but is itself "papery." So the spider isn't just, or really, a spider. She "should have run." Is there a tinge of defensiveness? Is the spider-killer saying, well, she shouldn't have squared up to me if she didn't want to be killed? It's how police officers often characterize their encounters with Black people, after murdering them. Or they say, "He *shouldn't* have run."

The parataxis, the repeated "and"s—"And she scared me / And I smashed her"—suggest an instinctive reaction. Something biased, immediate, and from the amygdala. Not a decision—"I don't *think*"—but a reflex. But really, "I don't think" begins a new, final sentence: "I don't think / I'm allowed / To kill something / Because I am / frightened." What touches me about this poem is how, having suggested breathlessly that our prejudices determine our behavior at a preconscious level, it then implies that the impulse to "think" harder can also come, as it were, naturally. The speaker is compromised but in a way that allows for multiple, conflicting thoughts. A world of race-relations is brilliantly contracted into simple phrasing, about an ordinary, seemingly insignificant, encounter. Fear is no excuse for violence. But is *all* violence motivated by fear; is this the most powerful critique of it available to us (the redescription of violence, that is, that violent people most dislike)?

---

I AM WRITING ABOUT SPIDERS to write about fear; and the feeling, of being shattered into a thousand pieces, while still presenting—like a mosaic—to the world a picture of coordinated wholeness.

My wife asked me once, do you know whenever you sleep on your side, you hug yourself? I asked her, where are my arms supposed to go? Before considering two, related, psychological concepts: *hypervigilance* and *self-holding*, and their role in my Sri Lankan Tamil, intergenerationally fraught, family, and—I suspect—the lives of many immigrants and people of color. It's the feeling that if we aren't always holding on to ourselves, we'll fly apart. Is it that the world is ready to smash us, into said pieces? Or is there an explosiveness within our very bodies—like the power which threw stars and dark matter every which way, at the Big Bang—requiring containment?

When I put my arms around myself, literally or figuratively, like that spider curled into a ball, it reminds me I'm *still there*; as I might, leaving the house, pat my thigh to check the keys in my pocket, then my breast pocket for the bulge of my wallet (with, inside it, forms of identification confirming who I am). The act of self-supervision, this perpetual touching of a nervous place within yourself, comes to be equated with life itself. When you're *not* at it, you're in a void.

Letting go, unclenching, feels increasingly unreasonable. You're that spider on its thread, bundled, unmoving. But the spider is dead. When we get to feeling this way, are we truly alive? Perhaps we misunderstand aliveness, associating it too wholly with self-consciousness; underrating, then, those stretches of self-forgetful intensity, losing yourself in the moment, where our deepest joys abide. From the hypervigilant perspective, those experiences resemble death not life, because life has become falsely aligned with the clinging ego, becoming exquisitely conscious of itself through assessing one's environment for threats.

It is the perpetual search for an impossible security.

—

JOHN KEATS DIED at twenty-five of tuberculosis (which had also killed his mother and brother). His poetry is often read in terms of his impending death—the premonition, that he wouldn't finish what he had started—

When I have fears that I may cease to be
    Before my pen has gleaned my teeming brain,
Before high-pilèd books, in charactery,
    Hold like rich garners the full ripened grain;
When I behold, upon the night's starred face,
    Huge cloudy symbols of a high romance,
And think that I may never live to trace
    Their shadows with the magic hand of chance;
And when I feel, fair creature of an hour,
    That I shall never look upon thee more,
Never have relish in the faery power
    Of unreflecting love—then on the shore
Of the wide world I stand alone, and think
Till love and fame to nothingness do sink.

Is there a different way of reading this sonnet? When the pandemic hit, and we were separated for two years from our families overseas, the more or less constant anxiety I inherited from my parents morphed into what psychologists call *rumination*: like a cow chewing and chewing the cud, my mind dwelt uncontrollably on smarting memories, actions taken in error, burned bridges, and a thousand possible dooms on the horizon: the unrevisable past and the undependable future. These thoughts returned out of the blue—often with no clear trigger, as if my brain were spontaneously self-sabotaging. Ludwig Wittgenstein wrote that "the world of the happy man is a different one from that of the unhappy man." I didn't know, falling asleep, which version of me would turn up in the morning. A day of sunshine, on Walden Pond, with the glitter of the green water walked around, and my wife's hand nestled in mine, could be blocked out—the happiness of the moment extinguished—by unrelenting cognitive noise. Even should I persuade myself out of a particular worry, it would always come back.

Keats's poem is not about death. It's about rumination over the *thought* of death. It also speaks to the anxiety of this high-achieving South Asian immigrant, in its sense both of the poet's powers and of his fear those powers may go unexpressed, canceled by his death—a more terrible loss than it would be simply to die if one *weren't* on such a sacred mission. Let me explain.

If we remove the center of Keats's sonnet—sonnets are often love poems, but the woman in question gets but a brief cameo here—we find the plain statement: "When I have fears that I may cease to be / . . . then on the shore / Of the wide world I stand alone, and think / Till love and fame to nothingness do sink." In the US, I'm surprised by the euphemisms for death innovated by a culture phobic of mortality: *died* became *passed away* which then became *passed.* My Sri Lankan family discusses death all the time. On Facebook, a relative shares a cartoon showing a mother with a child in her womb; then, her infant in her arms; the child, now an adult, appears, carrying her aged parent on *her* back; finally, the adult daughter holds the mother's urn. My mother loves to plan her own funeral ("I want it to be a celebration!"); she begins conversations with the ringing phrase, "When I am dead and gone . . ."

Keats never visited the US, though his brother George moved with his wife across the Atlantic and started a failed business. Their correspondence touched me deeply during the pandemic, when I couldn't see my parents or my sister in the flesh (couldn't touch them, literally), though they could watch me lecture on Keats online, and at one point tear up, knowing they were, in a sense, there.

In his first line, Keats *sounds* American—euphemistic, that is; he daren't name death, he uses more words than are necessary. "Fears that I may cease to be" puts the point flowerily. Though the phrasing is also necessary to the sonnet form—it's a line of rhymed, iambic pentameter—so we might hear this plodding line in terms of a *process of thought* Keats wills into motion, to counter a different kind of, more helplessly involuntary, thinking, experienced as entrapment.

"When I have fears that I may cease to be . . . "; "When I am dead and gone."

—

WHEN I WAS a depressed teenager, refusing school and hiding in my room, my mum bought me a self-help book (with an awful rainbow on the cover) called *Stop Thinking and Start Living*. Thrown out my bedroom window, it landed in a tree. Luckily, she never asked after it.

South Asians, as discussed, often pressure their children to excel. I have seen in family after family this extraordinary pressure either forge a child into a precocious diamond—or crush them. Among my brown peers, I see many superstars and dropouts; only a few in between, just going about their day.

Is it terrible to say that what I want most for my son, Frank, is a life of ordinary happiness? I ran so he could walk.

University professors, and poets, spend much time thinking, and sometimes it is painful, a question, even with scholarly research, of peering deep into oneself. So why would a South Asian parent, wanting her child to stop skipping school, and achieve a cavalcade of A grades, give him a book about how to stop thinking?

> I stand alone, and think
> Till love and fame to nothingness do sink.

"Thinking" has two meanings. We consider creative and scientific and philosophical *thought*—cognition—separate from such degraded, merely neurotic, repetitious, *over*thinking as self-help books address. This second kind of thinking is really worrying, catastrophizing, living too exclusively in the past or a dreaded future. It is, to reapply the term, *rumination*, which so inhabits and inhibits Keats, that when his mind is stuck in its cycle, nothing—neither "love" nor "fame"—means anything anymore.

—

TWO DEFINITIONS OVERLAP. We would like to consider the poet, scientist, philosopher, different from the anxious person postulating disasters. The start of Keats's failed epic, *The Fall of Hyperion*, hastens to make distinctions:

Fanatics have their dreams, wherewith they weave
A paradise for a sect; the savage too
From forth the loftiest fashion of his sleep
Guesses at heaven: pity these have not
Trac'd upon vellum or wild Indian leaf
The shadows of melodious utterance.
But bare of laurel they live, dream, and die;
For Poesy alone can tell her dreams,
With the fine spell of words alone can save
Imagination from the sable charm
And dumb enchantment.

Recent political upheavals, connected to our internetification, show us that human beings are not the rational actors presumed by economists. We are irrational, or, rather, nonrational; less likely to be changed in our views by argument than by powerful emotional experiences. Countless "fanatics" have, in these tempestuous times, created "a paradise for a sect," hypnotizing into conformity subcultures siloed against wider conversations. Worrying that the two kinds of thinking—philosophical creativeness, and obsessive neurosis—may be inseparable, Keats distinguishes the healing power of poetry from the destructiveness of "dumb enchantment." His blank verse—iambic pentameter without rhyme, in which one of his heroes, John Milton, wrote his own epic, *Paradise Lost*—allows syntax to run unimpeded from line to line, generating complex ideas, especially at the endings of lines: the word "save," for instance, takes great weight. "Poesy alone can tell her dreams, / With the fine spell of words alone can save . . . " As he goes on, we realize that it is imagination which is to be saved from its bad opposite. But for a moment, it seems as if only poetry can save us.

"Wild Indian leaf": the pity is not that people who looked different from Keats and lived elsewhere in the world did not have their own literature, but that so many works are lost to us, through either time or conscious destruction—the 1981 arson, for instance, of the library at Jaffna, with its irreplaceable Tamil works really inscribed on palm leaves (it is said the roundness of Tamil script evolved so as to not tear those wild, but also delicate, leaves)—or lost another way, through our unawareness of, our obtuseness unto, creativities unlike our own.

Keats defends one form of imagination against another: he insists creativity is linked to truth and to justice, not delusion and solipsistic fantasy. His egalitarian politics—the idea that everyone is equal, and has something to say—collides with the Romantic view of the poet as a special person exalted above others, but in a better way than tyrannical nobles and kings. Returning to the sonnet, it is impossible to parse its anxieties except as those of a person who knows that he is special, but has begun to experience that difference as not a blessing but a curse—a great, almost unendurable, responsibility. The poet of "teeming brain" fears their intellectual harvest will never occur; that the "magic hand of chance," such as could transform a thought glimmering in the sky into sustained creative work, will never alight on his shoulder; in the deeps of passion, he is horrified by the thought of never seeing again the woman he loves, and of never being truly, reciprocally, loved by her.

*Of course* it is in the moments of highest happiness, or

most intense self-expression, that we obsess over joys canceled, expression thwarted.

—

KEATS KEPT ME ALIVE as a teenager. One accusation aimed at him—I disagree—is that his talk of beauty and feeling and art shrugs aside history.

On the contrary: Keats's poetry has been crucially nourishing, at times when I feel put upon and set upon—often in response to my activism. I speak of dire stretches of sleeping badly, when my nervous gut gives me bad breath, and out of paranoias of gloom my one, primary, ruminative habit mercilessly resurfaces. When, that is, I begin to pick aggressively with my fingernail at my thumb, both when awake and asleep. It bleeds: the blood dries, leaving patches of sore, woebegone cerise, and a ragged yellowy unhealed edge.

Nick Walker, the autistic activist, says we all have what are demonized, in autistic people like my son and my wife, as "stims": she says that to "neuroqueer" oneself is to enfranchise these tendencies, restoring their place in your life. My finger goes on working at my thumb, doing what it can to regulate a welter of sensations. But in a combat phase, so many dimensions of one's being are flattened (one of the arguments of this book is that this may *sometimes* be why we pick fights, personal and political—to avoid looking deeply into ourselves). Loud noises become unbearable (those bowling alleys my son loves); my speech degrades into either a yelping hyperassertiveness, an interminable thinking-aloud about what interests me, or a silence gone hard.

Sometimes I hold firm so I can say and do the things,

publicly and privately, that I must. But at what cost? Political struggle may seem to require that one shrink oneself down, into a creature of pure, single-minded purpose. My nuances are erased. For me and many others it is exhausting to have to explain, to fight for, minoritized styles of being—yet again: work we aren't paid for (and which may endanger us at work), that often occurs behind the scenes, that is unglamorous and snaggy and substantially different from the big controversies that explode on social media and are cynically simplified by proponents of culture wars. There accumulates a resentment, at *having* to play this role, losing one's aliveness to the necessity of shouting through a megaphone.

The old idea of poetry as consolation is unsalvageable, because it sounds like escapism: reconciling oneself to the status quo. But Keats felt literature did help and heal, and not in a narcotically numbing way. He has always been there for me. Reading him, I feel parts of me I've had to put aside—simplify, to the point of erasure—returning to life. This is why, when he writes of poetry as a nook or shade or bower, or a renewing feast, or a balm, I don't find it escapist at all:

> A thing of beauty is a joy for ever:
> Its loveliness increases; it will never
> Pass into nothingness; but still will keep
> A bower quiet for us, and a sleep
> Full of sweet dreams, and health, and
>     quiet breathing.
> Therefore, on every morrow, are we wreathing
> A flowery band to bind us to the earth,
> Spite of despondence, of the inhuman dearth

Of noble natures, of the gloomy days,
Of all the unhealthy and o'er-darkened ways
Made for our searching: yes, in spite of all,
Some shape of beauty moves away the pall
From our dark spirits.

The first line of *Endymion* is one of the most famous in all of poetry. But we miss the undercurrent of anxiety behind these assertions, which are brave, even last-ditch, insistences—refusals of cynicism and the easy superiority achieved through preemptive disappointment. The line-division amplifying "never," and the three stresses, *still will keep*, aren't complacently triumphalist: this is a shareable form of hope, indispensable when the odds are against us. "Yes, in spite of all": Keats's long second sentence lists the counterforces of negation, the reasons for giving up, before asserting the inevitability of, not goodness or success or strength, but "beauty": the unpredictable otherness of the world, whose gift is to astonish.

Keats advocated for "diligent indolence," his version of William Wordsworth's "wise passiveness." If you try to control everything, if you don't allow surprises to happen, this may feel like safety but closes off the future. Keats wants us creatively on our toes, getting up every day (remember Dwibedy's blue boy) keen to nurture our bonds:

Therefore, on every morrow, are we wreathing
A flowery band to bind us to the earth

"A flowery band" sounds precious—Keats at his mawkish worst. But only for a split second, before "band" comes up against "bind." As one vowel sound gives way to another, and two near-identical words collide, it seems to me to mean—not less than everything. It is the effort one makes "on every morrow," to construct a new, perpetually shifting, relation to the world (Dwibedy's blue boy!): it is that determined, though not strident, purposiveness running deeper even than consciousness, to the point where, looking at the blood oozing from my thumb, I am pressed to recognize myself not only in that antic tic, but also in the unconscious styptic powers that slowly heal the skin, sewing together (with an invisible needle that some part of me knows how to thread) what was previously sundered. Rather than considering myself a tiny spotlight located just behind my throbbing eyes, I realize—reading these lines of Keats's *Endymion*—that I am my whole body: to fall asleep, waken, heal, to grow (gray) hairs, to blink and breathe, are also things I do, just as Keats says that poems should come to a poet either as the leaves to a tree or not at all. Something abides, below and more real than the grasping contentiousness that generates much of our culture. Speaking of the humane creative work we all do every day simply by existing, Keats asks if a politics can be retrieved from it. That is the challenge: to relearn to trust, to entrust oneself to, this process of "wreathing" which—given Keats's curious verb tenses—appears simultaneously passive and active, and even constraining. His poetry acknowledges that we are creatures of change, for whom there is no permanence except death (that "wreath" for a funeral, hidden inside "wreathing").

# *Victim and accused*

In 2017, I once again visited Sri Lanka with my parents. It had never previously felt safe to leave the tourist zones down south for the north, and the cities of Trincomalee and Batticaloa, where my parents were born (listed as containing the most widowed families, come the war's end). In Jaffna, where you're still surrounded by buildings ruined by bullets, and concrete turned (in the metaphor of the Sri Lankan poet Jean Arasanayagam) by bomb damage into Jackson Pollock drip-paintings, we found between a temple and a shop selling car seats a steel-roofed shack, with, strung across the entrance and the makeshift walls, countless laminated photographs of missing people. Youths. Most male, but there were also women, and children as young as ten. A teenager stared intensely at the lens, a waterfall of black, wild hair obscuring her left, bared shoulder. The Tamil text at the bottom of each image gave the name and contact details of their family; jostling for room, some of the posters were fastened to the corrugated roof.

We entered that space of women—Tamil—in the shade.

Most had gray in their hair, even those lying on the bare, lumpy ground. As soon as we entered, they rose and arranged a circle of chairs, with the expeditiousness of an army unit or a team of cheerleaders. Following the war, their people had never been returned. The government promised that the army and navy would release records, so families would know at last, at least, if their children had survived. This hadn't happened.

A vociferous woman (her face stern, with protrusive cheekbones) handed me a sweat-stained sheet of A4. She'd Photoshopped together images of a family—father, mother, two children—and the effect was telling, as if these people never occupied the same space at the same time, but were always destined to separate (the ink had run too, the blacks were green). All of them were likely dead: I saw it in her eyes. She wore a blue sari, tied her silver hair back in a hard bun, and announced: "We want our children returned to us in the same state they were in when they disappeared." Which meant she was at war not only with the government but with time itself.

Leaving, I was handed a photograph of a girl "taken" when she was eighteen. What did this mean, exactly? She could have been kidnapped off the street by the Tigers (short for the Liberation Tigers of Tamil Eelam), and turned into one of them—there were multiple all-female units, and indeed the LTTE recruited young people with boasts of gender equality. Then she may have died in battle, perhaps blowing herself up; or—though innocent—have been detained by the government and tortured to the point of death. She might be incarcerated to this day. Or was she sent to one of the camps where Tamils became political prisoners, with no access to legal representation, no prospect of justice? Did she find asylum abroad, or was she bused to the place an outdated census insisted was her home—an alien zone she fled—or maybe it was the right neighborhood, except her house was destroyed and her family had packed up and left? I see her in my mind's eye, assessing the damage, and setting off on her own—a journey taking her not toward but away from the people with whom she yearned to reunite.

The Tamil poet Cheran explains he has "no naive hope or belief that my poetry can turn the world upside down"; nevertheless, "words and imagination are my weapons. I have no other. There are several poems in my collections on disappearances evoking the friends I have lost." Even his more atmospheric, less clearly political, poems speak of yearning and loss. Lakshmi Holmström translates:

> Ask
> me,
> when the last train of the evening has gone
> and the railway lines shiver and break in the cold,
> what it is to wait with a single wing
> and a single flower.

Those women in the shack preferred to know once and for all that their children were dead, rather than go on waiting. In grief-work and trauma parlance, it's called closure. But it's also a basic kind of responsiveness and respect they were after, from the government: a commitment to a world of fact in which people are, or are not, dead, where they don't horribly hover in our minds between one state and another, like Schrödinger's cat. A place where their death, if that's the case, is recognized within national history, even if only by a statistic that few outside or indeed within the country will ever read.

—

A FEW YEARS AGO, I read poems at a festival. The auditorium, from the stage, was pitch-black: I couldn't see anyone. No faces, bodies, only the heat and shine of the spotlight on my face, shoulders, and the page on the lectern crawling with words that didn't seem mine. A language that—in that moment—felt as alien to me as Tamil. I spoke into a hollow void, and out of that disproportionate pause between speechlessness and speech (it was my turn to perform, to appear, the audience was waiting for me, it was wrong to delay, hem, haw, vanish into myself) emerged the roar of silence, of time itself passing, pushing me aside.

Searching for sentences that feel true, I realize I'm thinking of both a passage from George Eliot's *Middlemarch* and a trip taken as a teenager, with my parents, to Greece. I was abject: ashamed, those sunlit weeks, of my overweight brown body and acne-riddled face. There was one moment of relief, when my mother and I sat on the end of a pier past nightfall and became thankfully invisible to ourselves and to each other. All we heard was the loud roar of the invisible sea. "If we had a keen vision and feeling of all ordinary human life," writes Eliot, "it would be like hearing the grass grow and the squirrel's heart beat, and we should die of that roar which lies on the other side of silence."

—

THERE ARE MOMENTS when prose turns to poetry; when, reading a novel or a story, a sentence acts like a trapdoor. You tumble through, into a historical space previously beyond access, or (it could be one and the same) into a personal underworld whose existence you never suspected. The eye that skims from page to page is swapped out, you feel it has to be, for the ear that listens. Constructing a vast novel about life in a mid-nineteenth-century Midland town, Eliot writes a sentence of prose that's also a line of poetry. As sounds converge ("grass" and "grow," "hear" and "heart beat"), time itself becomes audible; "silence" begins to sing, rhyming with "like," "die," "lies," and "side." Reading this passage by a Victorian novelist, I'm once again with my mother at the end of that pier in Greece, past nightfall—listening, listening.

For Eliot—she's speaking of her heroine, Dorothea—our effect on others is "incalculably diffusive: for the growing good of the world is partly dependent on unhistoric acts; and that things are not so ill with you and me as they might have been, is half owing to the number who lived faithfully a hidden life, and rest in unvisited tombs." So much doesn't make it into the stories we tell, and read. So many acts go unmentioned, they aren't broadcasted or retweeted or cited, and this is as it should be, even if today's world places a premium on visibility and self-announcement. How little it's possible to actually attend to, though we yearn to tune in to a wider range! But we can live only through self-containment. We limit the field of our attention or have it limited for us, either by the apparatus of perception or by the culture we live in, whose news updates are typically about that culture: people like us, people not so far away.

—

THIS IS AN EXPERIMENT in talking about those women in that shack and what they felt, through talking about myself and how I once felt. It's an experiment in not being ashamed of my own "First World problems" (a phrase Teju Cole disparages, for it suggests Nigerians—in his example—live only from crisis to crisis, that they don't, also, get frustrated at their cellphones for crashing). This chapter risks a connection between the diasporic immigrant and those whose suffering is more intense than I'll ever know.

Onstage, I began to apologize for my poems. Poets shouldn't do this. It's one thing to be self-deprecating, and another to suggest your audience shouldn't have bothered coming out (paying, probably, to do so). As Eliot suggests, we've a limited amount of attention to give, so if you've nothing to say, get off the stage. I don't like the pressure on minority poets to be ostentatiously empowered. But I also feel the pressure to represent, with some kind of eloquence; this can fade, degrade, into an obligation to entertain; then you become a sort of minstrel figure. I was abject that day in Newcastle, asking forgiveness for my brownness, my presence onstage, for the content and style of my poems. Trying for contact, in that darkness, with a face I might see nod, or hear signal assent or appreciation, I felt in the end completely alone.

—

IN THE NORTH-EAST—in the run-up to, and the aftermath of, the referendum vote on Britain's exit from the European

Union—I experienced in the street the mushrooming racism of English culture. People didn't look at me in the same way anymore, nor, when I spoke, could they process what I was saying except through a scrim of media-fermented resentments (or, the determination to *not* be like this, to smile and nod at whatever the brown man said). Desperately seeking solutions—a style of invulnerability—I tried so hard to be likeable, biddable (which made me exploitable at work). I took to going around with an exaggerated smile on my face, as if strangers on the verge of violence could be preempted. One day a bloke actually parked up, beckoned me over, and complimented me on my good cheer. It was then I knew I'd become, as at that reading (dissolving my presence in jokes) the unthreatening minstrel I mentioned.

I don't want to ever turn into this person again. That's why this isn't *that* kind of memoir.

My wife and I had a terrible argument about house-buying, in the snooty area where we lived and no one spoke to us—where schoolboys snickered as they passed me on the street. "It's because we're the only renters," she said; I struggled to forgive her. It seemed we lived in two different worlds, that she couldn't understand changes in my life linked to convulsions in national culture. My students seemed to me, for I'd lost the confidence to draw them out, fiercely, determinedly passive. I wanted a conversation: they craved a mansplainer, perpetually sure of himself as I could never be, someone who'd keep them safe. When I did talk at length, they broke eye contact, typed everything down; should I ask a question, their faces went dead. I'd lost confidence. Students in their evaluations are consistently harder on women and minorities: they don't mean to be, I'm sure most aren't consciously racist (quite intensely the opposite, in my experience), but such are the subterranean workings of bias.

I felt, all in all, like the hallooing boy in Robert Frost's "The Most of It," calling out in the dark and waiting for an answer:

> He thought he kept the universe alone;
> For all the voice in answer he could wake
> Was but the mocking echo of his own
> From some tree-hidden cliff across the lake.
> Some morning from the boulder-broken beach
> He would cry out on life, that what it wants
> Is not its own love back in copy speech,
> But counter-love, original response.

He's a shade arrogant ("He thought he kept the universe alone"), in wishing to become self-sufficient. I have this in me, derived from our capitalistic, hypercompetitive culture, no doubt, and also from how my parents conceived of our immigrant place in it: when I tried to tell them how sad I'd become, they said, "Just keep achieving, writing things, stay ahead of the pack."

So was the problem in me, or outside me—or both?

—

WHEN YOU TRY TO TALK to people about racism you've experienced, they've ways of closing you down. Some are well documented, others less so. If minorities, and women, don't always speak up, it may be because they don't want to have a go at it only to be rebuffed. It may feel better not to say anything, so you can fantasize optimistically that if you did, the world would respond.

When a person of color tries to share their experiences, sometimes even those on the Left, white people who announce themselves anti-racists, don't listen or respond. Sometimes, when I tried telling friends, they, afraid of saying the wrong thing, didn't have the ears to hear. I'll call this phenomenon, riffing on white fragility, "white freeze": the moment or hideous duration where a person of color raises issues of race, and well-meaning white people seize up, go silent, lest they embarrass themselves by this micro-sojourn out of their own lane. This leaves said person of color feeling unvalidated and rejected. More silence. More darkness.

—

I'M THINKING STILL of those women petitioning the Sri Lankan army for news of their children, and being ignored; I'm trying to draw connections; you're free of course to find this a stretch. For an equivalent embarrassment (swapped rapidly for outrage) occurs when one compares sufferings of vastly different scale. I do want to provoke you a little here. Consider those celebrities who, during the coronavirus lockdown, posted videos of themselves crying in mansions they were unable to leave. People were incensed—especially online. But why, I wish to ask, are we so angry, racing to call one another out for obliviousness; why, in short, the cultural move toward using the experiences of some people to contradict the experiences of others? Is it truly a justice-instinct, or does this policing of sadness express only our uncertainty, which ferments into rage, concerning how we relate to each other, or don't, or can't, in a massively unequal multiculture?

—

THIS SITS CLOSE to what Reddit, the ubiquitous news aggregator and discussion site, calls "gatekeeping." I find a literary example, and a window on South African apartheid and its legacy, in Ingrid de Kok's "Small Passing," whose epigraph mentions " . . . a woman whose baby died stillborn, and who was told by a man to stop mourning, 'because the trials and horrors suffered daily by black women in this country are more significant than the loss of one white child.' " I suspect so much, here, is as familiar to you as it is to me. The gatekeeping of emotion; the imposed hierarchy of legitimate and illegitimate sufferings. Complications abound as a man, who couldn't experience this grief in the same way, tells a woman she's in the wrong, and I do wonder at de Kok, a white poet, for prioritizing gender over race: Would it make a difference to us if that man were definitely Black? If so, I still cannot imagine agreeing with him in the abstract, but I can imagine contexts where his utterance might emerge as a cry of understandable pain and frustration. Which leads me to wonder at the relation between de Kok's complex poem and her subtweet-resembling epigraph. What can poems do, that micro-forms of outrage (soundbites, tweets) cannot?

The poem strikes a moral stance, standing up for the bereaved woman by borrowing the man's voice and turning it inside out:

In this country you may not
suffer the death of your stillborn,
remember the last push into shadow and silence,
the useless wires and cords on your stomach,
the nurse's face, the walls, the afterbirth in a basin.
Do not touch your breasts
still full of purpose.
Do not circle the house,
pack, unpack, the small clothes.
Do not lie awake at night hearing
the doctor say 'It was just as well'
and 'You can have another.'
In this country you may not
mourn small passings.

In the movement from "you may not / suffer" to "you may not / mourn," de Kok addresses both private pain and the public display of it. The public dimension of grief, its validation by a community, is often essential for us to move on.

—

OF COURSE, THE TRAVAILS of a diasporic Sri Lankan Tamil, a second-generation immigrant, in an increasingly racist England don't *equate* to forced disappearances, torture and deaths "back home" (to use my parents' phrase). I sense the accusation; I make it myself: *You can't compare these things. You're not the same as those people.* How often has this guilty disparity, that is also a yearning to reconnect one's own pain with a family past, afflicted South Asians? Rhik Samadder, whose grandmother, like mine, was named Kamala—and whose war-displaced family eked out an existence in the outskirts of Calcutta—made his depression worse by comparing it with her more undeniable suffering:

> Where did this devastating force come from, and would I always be under its power? Unlike for my grandmother, the condition didn't feel like a response to a catastrophic event, unless it was one I had forgotten.

The notion of intergenerational trauma may help, tying what the immigrant child in the West feels now, to what their families went through (Bhanu Kapil analyzes, for instance, legacies of schizophrenia in the families of Indian and Pakistani survivors of the Partition). It is saddening, but also reassuring—restoring a sense of proportion, of cause-and-effect—to consider that one's depression may have "come from" the same place as one's family, that it is indeed a (delayed, deferred, disguised) "response to a catastrophic event," and thus a means of relating to a family history from which one would otherwise, living in the West, feel dislocated. It's unsurprising that, as he writes elsewhere, Samadder, like many of us, has "become interested in epigenetics, specifically the way trauma might be able to travel in gene expressions." But if we cannot find the scientific evidence, are we still to refuse connections between experiences—routes by which feeling might travel? We have to use what we have to understand others, even those who've attacked us, perhaps out of their own merited feelings of pain and insecurity. And the ability of the mind to augment its own torment means that no simple, one-to-one correspondence exists, between how much the world has bashed us and how much pain we feel.

So there I am, stood in the dark or sat before the silence of others, afraid no one's listening, that the world's growing more and more hostile; and there are those women in their shack, launching at a faceless wall of bureaucracy questions about their dead to which no one in power pays the slightest heed.

—

THE DARKNESS MY VOICE disappeared into onstage could to some extent be medicated away (I was put on antidepressants); it could be explained without reference to racism or the intergenerational terrors which, like a set of rogue genes, get passed down from immigrant parents to their children. My counselor suggested my mother was overattentive to me as an infant. (Except, this is to do with race, and being Tamil too, is it not? How hard it is, to unravel our histories.) As soon as I declared a need—maybe, even prior to this, before baby Vidyan began to cry—she rushed in to placate me. As a result, I never learned to entrust myself to the darkness which, should I only hold out, would conjure her, a duration in which I might, too, learn to self-soothe. Instead I came to feel that, without an immediate response, I must be alone.

Sleep-training Frank, it was agony to hear him wailing in the dark, and see him crying and writhing in seething, pixellated grayscale, on the baby monitor. Beyond loving my son, I identified with him. His feelings were so close to mine. I sat downstairs, in the light, while he sobbed upstairs, in the dark. Before he was born, my wife and I never thought we'd let our baby "cry it out": we agreed with writers like Penelope

Leach and Philippa Perry, who suggest that children left to sob in pitch-black, when they do eventually fall asleep, have simply given up on their parents, a decision affecting how empathetic they'll be later in life. But consoling Frank only made it worse: he had to be left to surmount this hurdle himself. We tried to be happy downstairs, watching television, though our eyes would relentlessly dart to the baby monitor.

This produced a deep guilt, that I'd like here to connect—again, an experiment—with the diasporic situation. In this model, Frank becomes like those women in Sri Lanka, struggling to be heard; my wife and I downstairs, in our cozily lamplit sitting room, resemble those of us in the West, quite unaware of atrocities in the Global South, and indeed enjoying luxuries predicated on the exploitation of those regions. Looking at the monitor and seeing Frank in pain and fear was like glancing at one's phone and reading of distant events one wishes in some way to mitigate, by getting angry about them, perhaps by opinionating online—feeling, all the while, an immense powerlessness to actually help.

—

IN DESPERATE TIMES, childhood horrors have ways of resurfacing. Alfred Tennyson, mourning his friend Arthur Hallam, describes himself as a hapless baby:

Behold, we know not anything;  
I can but trust that good shall fall  
At last—far off—at last, to all,  
And every winter change to spring.

So runs my dream: but what am I?
An infant crying in the night:
An infant crying for the light:
And with no language but a cry.

My parents, like many other immigrants, were overprotective. The overprotected child comes, first, to believe they're fragile; second, they decide the world is full of dangers (it is, but misidentifications are rife); finally, they may sense they're a risk to themselves and require permanent oversight. They seek out protector-figures, rituals keeping harm at bay; the Strange Situation—an experiment in which a mother leaves the room, and when she returns, her child may not go to her but instead attend ferociously to a toy, announcing silently that he doesn't need her—suggests that if distraction can be a neurotic symptom, so too can attention: a too-intent focusing on the task at hand. Self-loss through workaholism. Sometimes I wonder if even my ability to concentrate on a poem, to rediscover through it another way forward, has its root in some abyssal unease.

—

"EVERYTHING HAPPENS FOR A REASON," says my mother—her Hindu fatalism chiming uncannily with Tennyson's cobbled-together theology—and as a teenager this enraged me. "That's such a middle-class, privileged thing to say," I shouted, "what if your grandson Rahul was hit by a car and left in a wheelchair for the rest of his life? What would be the reason for that? And what about all those people who died in Sri Lanka?"

Objecting to global injustices, or inequalities closer to home, there's the danger—I see it in myself and my peers, and sometimes my students—of becoming locked in a position of righteous indignation. There is much to be angry about. But some rebels would rather keep the world as it is—so they can continue raging, so they have an identity—rather than change it. I don't wish to imprison myself in the grievance-posture of a teenager (a self-positioning that seems especially, addictively, available today). There's a brave moment—a moment one could object to—in Solmaz Sharif's *Look* where, discussing the invasion of Iraq and the killing of civilians, she suggests that she too, an Iranian American, has experienced war. Or rather, she has been "at war," as if she were a nation-state rather than an individual:

According to most
definitions, I have never
been at war.

According to mine,
most of my life
spent there.

The second stanza hasn't the confidence to really hammer home the equivalence. It's a clipped blurt, such as I, when unhappy, began to specialize in. Sharif suggests that war is both a state of mind and a place: "most of my life / spent *there*"; is she saying that, as the child of immigrants, she feels for their homeland too?

But radicals must, as with British South Asians in the eighties (and beyond), make "links"—turning to Anandi

Ramamurthy's extraordinary study, *Black Star*—"between their own struggles and international ones"; this is what made possible, once, "a strong anti-imperialist perspective. As Sivanandan had declared in 1987, 'for us South Africa was not "out there," it was in our kitchens.'"

—

THERE IS—TO RECAPITULATE—A trend now, of leaping to criticize others, and ourselves, for comparing petty injuries with atrocities. I wonder if the critique of self-pity is itself laced with self-pity; if, damning appropriation, we're rushing to cover up in ourselves emotions that dwarf, in their overweening rancor, any one reference point or, as T. S. Eliot has it (criticizing Hamlet for this), an "objective correlative." If, returning to Keats, and what he says elsewhere in his letters, "imagined grievances" can hurt more than real ones (a prompt to action in the moment, these have a built-in end point), then intense feelings deserve our understanding, even if they can't be securely traced to undeniable, large-scale, trauma. And so Sharif suggests that as an Iranian American woman subject to both interpersonal racism and state scrutiny, she is at war.

Tennyson was a racist—ranting to Gladstone that people in the colonies deserved to be shot. He's also not the most fashionable poet ("Alfred Lawn Tennyson," James Joyce called him). Because my father memorized and learned to love Tennyson as part of his colonial education at a Jesuit school in Batticaloa, I obviously argued, growing up, that Tennyson was mellifluous sham. But I was teaching recently a poem by Sujata Bhatt that mentions him, and my student Sophia Gatzionis made a wonderful point, about the transferability between cultures of unspecific melancholia: feeling-states which in Tennyson seem overkill, but may clarify for the reader a very different sort of life. In other words, it's precisely *because* Tennyson's emotions are excessive, his self-pity without terminus, that he's able to communicate across divides. We see this in Bhatt's poem about her grandfather, "Nanabhai Bhatt in Prison":

> The next day, he lands in prison again:
>
> thrown in without a trial
> for helping Gandhiji,
> for Civil Disobedience.
>
> One semester in college
> I spent hours picturing him:
> a thin man with large hands,
> my grandfather in the middle
> of the night, in the middle of writing,
> between ideas he pauses to read
> from Tennyson, his favourite—
>
> *A hand that can be clasped no more—*
> *Behold me, for I cannot sleep,*
> *And like a guilty thing I creep*
> *At earliest morning to the door.*
>
> What did he make of the northern trees?
> The 'old yew', the chestnut . . .
> and the strange season of falling leaves
> that comes every year—

Did he spend hours trying
to picture it all?

What galled me about my father's love of Tennyson was that it felt like an infatuation with the Glory of English Literature itself—a fossilized idea of white greatness. How else could he leap the distance between his world and Tennyson's?

But it's precisely this adventure of the imagination for which Bhatt's poem clears a space. She thinks her grandfather was capable of it: she takes his love of canonical British literature seriously (mentioning, also, that "as a student in Bombay / he saved and saved / and lived on one meal a day for six months / just so he could watch / the visiting English Company / perform Shakespeare"). Who are we to accuse him of false consciousness? The overflow of Tennyson's grief for his dead friend, feelings connected with those which, in poems that *aren't* elegies, he indulges to excess—all this could be felt over again (differently but similarly) by an Indian man jailed for his politics. It spoke to him: *In Memoriam A.H.H.*, that long, tendentious, uneven, mournfully recircling poem, in the work it does on the page with Arthur Hallam's death, created an atmosphere of feeling in which Nanabhai Bhatt, imprisoned thousands of miles away and alive in another century, and who never knew Hallam, could nevertheless share.

Sujata Bhatt "spent hours" in college picturing her grandfather; she wonders, did he "spend hours" picturing Tennyson's landscapes—using the same word, the same verb, as Sharif: "most of my life / *spent* there." To spend time is to use up our lives. And Bhatt suggests there's no better expenditure than hours or even years of trying to understand other people:

And I spent hours
picturing his years in prison:
Winter 1943;
it is dark in his cell.
He is sixty years old.
I see him
sitting cross-legged on the floor
and I wonder what he knew
by heart, I wonder
which lines gave him the most comfort.

Thinking of those Tamil women—they must imagine obsessively the horrors their vanished loved ones went through, possibly in prison, like Nanabhai Bhatt—I hear an emphasis differentiating "hours" in the first line from "years" in the second. This is where the poet recognizes the difference in stature between her grievances and her grandfather's: it's the difference between mere hours and sheer years.

I also pause at the line-ending on "knew." Nanabhai Bhatt knew Tennyson by heart (he didn't have a copy of the poems in his cell). But "I wonder what he knew" reaches deeper. Rather than presume she knows better than her Tennyson-loving, Shakespeare-obsessed, Anglophile grandfather, Bhatt wonders if he actually "knew" something that she, to this day, doesn't: that you don't, and I don't.

She also writes bilingual poems, where the italicized material would be Gujarati: in this case, the foreign substance in the poem is a stanza from Tennyson. How much foreignness, strangeness, can a poem—can any of us—admit into ourselves, into our lives and behaviors, without losing what's essentially us? Or is there no essential me (or you)—

only this space where ideas, languages, power circuits, cross? Best, then, to keep our borders open.

*And like a guilty thing I creep.*

—

IN *THE SEASONS OF TROUBLE*, her book about the Sri Lankan civil war, Rohini Mohan contrasts the lives of detainees subjected to torture, sexual abuse, and coercion with those of loved ones trying to locate them. Mohan also outlines the attempts of relatives to continue living from day to day, turning, to this end, their petitionary visits to the relevant authorities into a type of religious ritual, a gesture of observance rather than a genuinely investigative claim—they learned long ago no response was forthcoming. Hindu fatalism plays its role: the idea that all is in the hands of the gods is an idea chronically accessible (as psychologists say of our obsessive thoughts) to people suffering the whims of faceless authoritarian power. Thousands of civilians died when shelled by the army or fired upon by the Tigers for trying to remove themselves from the northern war zone. But even those in the south, observes Frances Harrison, "lived with the constant threat of suicide bombers, terrified even to let their children walk to school."

My parents and sister left Sri Lanka in the seventies: I was born in Leeds in 1984, the year after the war began. Our family's great fear took, takes, this form: *something bad is coming; what we just escaped can still touch us.* In particular, through my uncle, who stayed behind. He'd been imprisoned too, supposedly for helping the Tamil Tigers. In 1983, he was a GP in Trincomalee, the small town on the east coast where he and my mother were born. A middle-class Tamil (this is important, he'd never have made it otherwise), he tried to leverage what authority he had, accepting a reconciliatory role in the community—though it brought on threats.

As a member of the "People's Committee," he was instrumental in securing the release of several youths accused of anti-state activities in 1983; the rioting of what is now known as Black July saw armed personnel arrive at his clinic—also his home—and begin firing through the front door. The whole family, including his mother, my grandmother, had to leap the fence and huddle in an empty plot before returning to their looted home in the morning. What was remarkable was the sudden (or so it seemed) switch from civility to murderousness, and back again. Sinhalese and Tamil communities lived side by side, they were friends. Then—what changed?—buses were set on fire with people still in them, tires were forced around Tamil men, containing their arms so they couldn't get away, and these too were set on fire. Then—after it was over—you went round to your neighbors for tea, and found it served out of your own cups, gone missing during the looting.

Thirteen soldiers had been killed near Jaffna by the LTTE; a mob, in response, convened at their funeral and distributed (gained from the police and army, who were complicit) documents identifying Tamil businesses and homes. Chandragupta Amarasinghe's photographs of the events of Black July were suppressed until 1997; nor was it possible to track him down and acquire the rights to reproduce them here. Yet it is vital, because of the Sri Lankan government's refusal to admit to the war crimes and other atrocities committed against Tamils, that this history is recovered. So I urge you to find these photographs online (where they are freely available), and I'll describe two at length.

In the first, we see a rioter, arms upraised, in front of a street-fire of Tamil goods and vehicles. The flames look in the black-and-white image so absolutely white it's as if reality is being erased. A smear, a smudge, an injury to the negative: it looks less like flame than a resistance within the very event, to representation. (Again, I think of the obstacles to reproducing the photograph in these very pages.) The man's posture reminds me of the "war victory" sculpture we saw on our travels up-country, a soldier depicted on a plinth with four sculpted lions (the roaring animal on the Sri Lankan flag; *Sinhalese* means "lion-people"), one at each corner.

We don't have to, however, concentrate on the man in his white undershirt and striped sarong who, recognizing the presence of the cameraman, makes himself the center of the spectacle. In front and slightly to one side stands another, looking less carefully posed (one arm has disappeared) and uncertain, as do the figures to the left with their arms crossed and wearing expressions of restive enjoyment, but also chagrin. It could be that they weren't ashamed before Amarasinghe showed up. But I'd like to think that even within the mob there were hesitations, moments of ambivalence, men and women picking up weapons, then putting them down, and wondering what on earth they were doing.

---

ANNE RANASINGHE, BORN ANNELIESE KATZ, lived through—as a Jewish child in Germany—the *Kristallnacht*, or "night of broken glass," a pogrom against her people. She also witnessed the arson of the synagogue at Essen. Marrying a Sri Lankan, she was present for Black July. Godwin's law is an internet joke about flame wars (as they used to be called), and how, the more heated an argument gets, the more likely it is that one party will compare the other to Hitler. Nazism and the Holocaust represent absolute evils, and to invoke them feels excessive, as when Sylvia Plath, in "Daddy," compares that patriarch to a Nazi and herself to a Jew. But Ranasinghe's unique cross-cultural experience inspires, in "July 1983," a poem daring to find in one atrocity the means for understanding another:

I used to wonder
about the Nazi killers,
and those who stood and watched the killing:

does the memory
of so many pleading eyes
stab like lightning through their days and years

and do the voices
of orphaned children
weeping forlornly before dying

haunt their nights?

Both the killers and the German bystanders are guilty: Ranasinghe moves from the past into the present tense, wondering if Nazis lived mentally, afterward, a version of the trauma they inflicted on others.

are their nights sleepless—
has the agony and anguish and

the blood and terror and pain
carved a trail in their brain
saying: I am guilty. Never again. . . .

More precisely, she says that she "used to wonder" about this, like Sujata Bhatt spending hours picturing her grandfather's situation. The past tense means she, Ranasinghe, stopped doing this. Perhaps as war criminals aged, were tried, and died; or once she decided there was no hope for, in them, any evolving awareness of what they did; could the change of tense register her move from one country to another as an opportunity for terminating her speculations?

Unfortunately, having moved to Sri Lanka, she finds the event, or a version of it, has rearrived like a traumatic memory. With emphatic anger—making connections, finding rhymes—she writes out of a *now* that, were it not for her poem, and Amarasinghe's photographs, might have faded into a footnote, a statistic:

Forty years later
once more there is burning
the night sky bloodied, violent and abused

and I—though related
only by marriage—
feel myself both victim and accused,

(black-gutted timber
splinters, shards and ashes
blowing in the wind: nothing remains)—

flinch at the thinnest curl of smoke
shrink from the merest thought of fire
while some warm their hands at the flames.

The interjection about being "related / only by marriage" compares with Sharif wondering if she too has experienced war; also with my worry, about how to "relate" to world traumas without taking them over. "Related" refers to actual familial relation, even as the poem wonders if the two crises are really "related," though one is taking place—the words almost, again, rhyme—"forty years *later*." The transposition of Jewish and Tamil trauma, the past and the present, is felt in Ranasinghe's floating adjectives, "bloodied, violent and abused." Describing the flame-tinged smoke-filled sky of Colombo, she sees the firmament as, first, bleeding like a Tamil, then, violent like the mob, then abused, again like those Tamils (or Jewish people). I linger to stress how the sky represents Ranasinghe's own impure position: a mixture she bravely confronts, rather than announcing herself as wholly one of the good and true and victimized. A particular kind of historical consciousness is trying in this poem to come into being: subject positions merge and easy distinctions are upended.

The poet feels both "victim and accused." The rhyme is powerful because, while she has married into this situation, her husband isn't Tamil and she worries she's on the wrong side, though her gut reactions, shaped by a terrified Jewish childhood in Germany, are those of the "victim," the survivor who sees violence and instinctively flinches and shrinks from it, rather than seeking immunity through identification with the aggressor. The mixed time signatures in the parentheses (the fire ongoing; also, a view of what's left afterward, that is, "nothing") suggest a consciousness untethered from particular horrors into an all-encompassing territory of fear.

—

THE BONFIRE OF TAMIL goods isn't Amarasinghe's most famous picture of Black July. That'd be his portrait (the right word, I think: it's revelatory, painterly, a window on the soul) of a Tamil man stripped naked and about to be beaten, possibly to death. It's one of those photographs where, as with Kevin Carter's notorious image of a starving Sudanese child eyed by a vulture, one mildly despises the photographer for not intervening. Between the blurred gaiety of the men on the right and the abject nudity of the man on the left, it feels the witness must jump in, barring the way. The concrete step the Tamil man sits on seems to absorb his thighs like memory foam—starved-looking, he takes on the entrenched victimhood of that Sudanese child, or the photographs of Jewish people in concentration camps. But it's important to remember that, minutes earlier, he would've been fully clothed: we don't discover in this photograph anything essential about his personality. Instead, he becomes exemplary, a picture of, as Shakespeare puts it in the voice of Lear, "unaccommodated man," who is "no more but such a poor, bare, forked animal as thou art."

I put it to you that there are moments of your life when you *did* feel something of what the man in the picture does (if you like, we can separate the man photographed, iconic, from the actual person whose life isn't recorded). When you felt abject, wholly alone; when your terror began to morph into the learned helplessness of an animal that, with no other options, stops running and fighting and goes simply still. Because of this, you and I, though we haven't (speaking for myself) survived such an atrocity, have a way into this photograph deeper than connoisseurship and more prolonged than a sad, knowing shake of the head. This is a confrontation with man's inhumanity to man, or whatever soundbite one might use to wrap things up and move on from horrors so extreme as not only to jar with one's everyday life but also to actively contradict it, rendering our happiest moments unrealities, evasions of what has now been revealed as the baseline of human experience.

Yes, even though you haven't been stripped naked by a mob, beaten by them, had everything taken, and even though you're likely not Tamil, look at the picture. Think your way into it. Try.

---

I WISH I COULD SUBSTITUTE, for those women in the shack meeting me and my mother—although she could at least speak with them, weep with them—a journey through time, and a chance for them to meet Anwar Ditta. Ditta changed the course of British history in the eighties by forcing the government to recognize that her children stranded abroad in Pakistan *were* her children, and deserved to be allowed into the country. Campaigning, networking, she gave speeches of immense power:

> I am willing to give a medical test. I am willing to give a skin test. I am willing to go on a lie detector to prove that they are my children. . . . I didn't know English law. . . . I thought if I go to England and get a job and buy a house and we have got settled, then I'll call the children. I didn't want my children to suffer.

Ditta "learnt," observes Anandi Ramamurthy, "to highlight the way in which her own case reflected the injustice of a system that appeared to criminalise her and victimise her for being black"; her campaign "liaised with trade unions, left organisations, religious organisations."

I wish further solidarities were possible—crossing oceans, decades, to unite that heroically struggling mother in mid-century England with these Tamil women still fighting for their families in Sri Lanka. What might they say to each other?

—

TWO YEARS AFTER BLACK JULY—as I turned one, in Leeds, in the north of England—and five days before Deepavali, the festival of lights, my uncle was arrested along with several other Tamils, and, detained at the naval headquarters, accused of making payments to the Liberation Tigers of Tamil Eelam. His life could have been over. But he wasn't like that naked man on the curb. He was protected—by connections, and by his class. A member of the Sinhalese security forces whom he'd previously treated at his medical practice spoke up on my uncle's behalf.

While detained, my uncle was allowed to remain in this man's private quarters, and one night, when he had to leave to deal with rioting elsewhere, he even handed him a pistol and asked him to mind his two small children. It was through another connection—the power of his politically influential father-in-law—that my uncle was eventually released; returning home, he was advised to leave the country, for there was now a strong chance that, in a reprise of Black July, he and his family would be targeted. They lived for three years in exile in Tamil Nadu. My parents visited them, taking me: ill throughout with food poisoning, I remember nothing of the stay.

—

I DO REMEMBER our later visits to my uncle's small flat in Colombo, where he lived with his wife, their two sons, and my grandmother—several people to one room. My aunt worked in IT: their only spare room was crammed with machines for her students. My strongest memories are of the nights when, during the daily official power outage, we lit candles and played carrom by their flickering light: you aim a counter at colored wooden discs, trying to get them into the board's pockets, as with a snooker or billiard table. Before playing, my uncle massaged talcum powder into the wood to keep it slick. I remember the smell of it, a sweet smell, and the reflection of the candles in his glasses. I idolized his good-naturedness. Unlike my father, my uncle isn't brooding, saturnine, or (I thought then) given to anger. He's a round, jolly man, despite what he went through, what his family went through.

I realized how essential to me this belief, passing into myth, had become, when my mother told me, just a few years ago, that my uncle once beat my cousin Balu with a belt when he misbehaved. How could this be? I couldn't imagine my uncle's happy face distorted in rage, the belt snapping through the air. Thinking of him, I remembered only carrom, his autodidacticism (he wrote to me about the theory that Shakespeare wasn't really the author of his plays), his love of photography and its high-tech equipment; the beautiful snapshots he took in Canada and Australia (where his sons now live) of both land and sea birds. I cherished the myth—incarnated in him—of a transcendently bumbling, oblivious, soft-hearted goodness which, if it got him through the horrors of the Sri Lankan civil war, would surely, if I could emulate it, protect me from discrimination in the UK.

—

THE SITUATIONS we live through change us—at least temporarily, if not for good. I look at my son Frank and the thought of hitting him makes me feel sick (but then, so did the idea before he was born, of leaving him to cry in the dark). One of my strongest childhood memories is of dashing down our hallway in Leeds, colliding with my father's knee and falling over—of his excessive concern, the tears in his eyes as he took me in his arms, asking repeatedly, "Did I hurt you?" Only years later did I learn that his father, my grandfather—whom I never met, who died before I was born, who is nevertheless the only person alive or dead I truly hate—used to beat him. Not for any reason: he'd just come home and for a laugh punch his son in the stomach.

At university, I had a girlfriend who struck out verbally and also physically, hitting me on two occasions, once with an open hand and once with closed fists, in the chest. When I told my father, those tears reappeared in his eyes. "Someone who hits you doesn't really respect you," he said. The look on his face was irrefutable—it was earned; behind it lay a history I was only just beginning to understand, a history that being attacked by the person in the world who was supposed to love me best perhaps even helped me, eventually, to fathom.

As a child my father once ran away from home. This is what Balu did too. The incident with my uncle and the belt occurred during that stretch in Tamil Nadu—after they were forced to flee Trincomalee by the events I've described. Suddenly they were poor: my grandmother, pensionless, depended on the family; my aunt became a seamstress to make ends meet. In a new country, a new situation, my cousin couldn't take it anymore: he disappeared. When he was brought back to the house, in that moment of uncertainty and fear, my beautiful, gentle uncle lost it. He took out his belt, shifting from victim to aggressor.

We speak of appropriation in the arts but there are more private, secret, appropriations. I took my uncle's tenderness, removed it from history, and, forcing a smile, tried to resemble the person I wanted him to be—so no one would hurt me. That's why the news about him disciplining my cousin meant so much: it contradicted the cardboard cutout I'd made of him, the grossly simplified angel I'd reduced him to for my own purposes. But that buoyant humor of his was never an evasion of those furies visited and inscribed upon Tamils. His love for his son, my cousin, has outlasted the mistake with the belt. I made a worse error, rewriting my uncle's life—because I wanted to rewrite mine.

# *Pandemic*

We moved to the US in January 2020. If we'd known we'd be separated from our families in England for two years by the pandemic and travel ban, we wouldn't have come. Snowdrifts of paperwork dominated our lives (only in February 2023 did we receive green cards)—and the real snow, three feet high and freezing diamond-hard overnight, was as dumbfounding as (to her) my mother's first English snowfall, when she moved to Yorkshire from Sri Lanka in the seventies. As it melted we walked our pram down the salubrious streets of Lexington, only to find the pavements—sidewalks—petering out without warning, since this was an area where if one did walk, it was along designated scenic trails.

We were housesitting—catsitting—really, hot-tub-sitting, maintaining the permanently active (whirring and foaming) ecological disaster plonked on a specially reinforced deck; marking conscientiously on an otherwise entirely empty calendar, with more photogenic cats on it, the days for augmenting with chemicals the ever-churning foam. Gradually our walks shifted to the bike path through the trees, where we stayed six feet from everyone with the same idea, wearing dust-masks retrieved from the garage. Eyeing warily the sign marking a battle between the settlers and the British—were we welcome here?—we pushed Frank amazing distances, reassured whenever someone smiled at us. Yet we could also roam for miles and see nobody at all.

We watched a lot of bad television. *Westworld*, beyond the first season. Morosely my wife and I asked each other: "Do you fancy another episode of Breasts?"—our name for it, because of the amount of female nudity, and the complacency of its packaging as empowerment. But time had to be killed. We didn't want to feel anything, wanted to become robots ourselves. With Frank asleep, time disappeared—we made it disappear—into a void, as if we could race to the end of this nightmare and resurface overnight into a virus-free world.

—

THERE ARE MOMENTS in dire shows, or films, or video games, of unexpected suggestiveness, even beauty. Some counterforce alleviates the tawdriness and stupor. Reading a poem by Zoë Brigley, I realize it's about a scene in *Westworld*. It reveals something momentous within what was previously unexceptional.

WESTERN UNION

Here's a story—not mine—of a woman out West,
not the American West as it is now, but

a place without time. Long ago, she shed her dress,
and now she wears a belt and boots, faces the men

round the campfire. Like Claudia Cardinale or
Katy Jurado in a film I once saw: *Nothing*

*you can do to me*, *not a thing*, *that won't wash off*
*with soap and water.* One man watches, and does

nothing. Another one behind her, encircling
with one arm: the other hand stabs, slices her open

from sternum to navel. She gasps at the wound:
not guts, but wire, pistons, circuits. Did you see

it too? The moment that told us what violation
meant: forced to look, to see nothing like flesh.

Brigley analyzes sexual violence in her poetry and her prose, and has taught an advocacy course in women's studies. When I asked her about this poem, she expressed disappointment at *Westworld*, but also suggested that "making women into robots is the ultimate way of commenting on how dehumanised they are":

> I thought that the moment when they cut her open and find her to be a robot was horrifying but strangely familiar. It stands in for any kind of violation and to violate someone we have to make them less than human. There is also the fact that now she has been violated, publicly shown to be a robot, [men] will reject her, and I guess I

related to that when I think about how men react sometimes when they find out that you are a survivor.

In *Westworld*, the woman in question is an older-model robot, not constructed like the others out of amorphous sci-fi gloop, but with mechanical workings. So it's also a moment where she is revealed as obsolete, out of date—sexist ideas about women aging become relevant.

—

WHEN JENNY AND I WATCHED this scene during lockdown, it felt both like a sexual wounding and as having to do with childbearing and childbirth. Dolores's womb is, so to speak, cut open and there is nothing there. The generative magic is absent, that men historically have envied (with feelings devolving into misogyny). The robot is also a barren woman. Jenny gave birth to Frank by emergency C-section, after over thirty hours of labor. I've never felt so powerless to help my wife, so utterly outside what was important, able to comfort her only with massages, cups of tea, and guided walks up and down the stairs of the hospital, supposedly to nudge Frank free of his stubborn perch inside her and out into the world. Hers was the most incredible feat of physical heroism. In the weeks after, I failed Jenny by finding it impossible to inject her every day, as was required, in the stomach. She had to do that by herself too. She had never seemed to me more formidable—urgent, tender, ingenious—as during those weeks when our baby changed our lives forever, and breastfeeding both exalted and exhausted her. She did have her friends in Birmingham, from work and the orchestra she played in, and her family only hours away, visiting in a trice.

—

NOW, IN MASSACHUSETTS, glancing anxiously between the television screen and Frank's baby monitor, she'd lost everything—I'd taken it from her; Jenny looked bereft. There was a growing pause every time I asked her a question. Facial expressions I didn't—this was before Frank's autism diagnosis, and before my wife's counselor suggested she is probably neurodivergent too—know how to interpret. Following me across the sea for the sake of my career, she was without a support network: disallowed a job, even a social security number, she, in a sense, didn't *exist*, as we soon discovered when creating bank accounts. Jenny had always spoken quietly. Now she couldn't make herself understood to others: people here asked her to repeat herself, and still misheard. I sensed her slowly disappearing (feeding Frank had made her very thin). Had emigrating and immigrating destroyed us? We began to really fight, as never before. The world shrank to just the three of us, in someone else's house, and a country that wasn't ours.

Jenny had lost, had taken from her, something beyond my understanding. I, never at home anywhere, feeling no real ownership over the English flats and wonky houses we rented, couldn't grasp what it was, to feel suddenly, not continuously and endurably, alien. I'm from a family of immigrants: for Jenny, crossing the pond was an aching violation. To watch her strip herself down, as it were, to her component parts, and rebuild—refusing (particularly around

Frank's diagnosis) the easier routes, of either total-convert-to-Americanness or prissily-embattled-Brit-abroad—has been, again, to witness a type of heroism. Something far more impressive than a female robot in a catsuit shooting men down in a supposedly empowering kill-montage.

—

AS JENNY AND I DRIFTED APART, into our figurative isolation-chambers—doing daily what we had to, for Frank, but with little flow of warmth back and forth—I examined the house in which we'd found ourselves. Exploring silently from room to room, sometimes with Frank asleep in my arms, while Jenny dozed off in the basement. Coming to a sight of snow through the window, or hearing of a sudden an unidentifiable creak or clang, I'd pause, feeling afresh how frail one's hold on both place and time could become. It was a four-floored Victorian, with evilly steep stairs—how many times, in my mind's eye, did I see Frank tumble out of my arms and helplessly down them, his small bones smashed?

To be at large in a stranger's house felt like a problem to solve. What was I there to do? I browsed the shelves of our absent hosts with my free hand, tracing the spines of books expressive of their lives, not mine. It was the sort of raid I've always been up to, a sort of literary breaking and entering. One could peer—through books, scandalously—into the wires, circuits, pistons, of the lives of others.

One day I read an unexpectedly nuanced discussion online—the sort you wish for more often, not sound and fury signifying nothing, or (worse) abuse flung like mud. Major Jackson wrote about Wallace Stevens seeing a photograph on the wall of Gwendolyn Brooks—Stevens was brought in to judge the National Book Award, a role she'd had previously—"Who's the coon?" he asked. And again: "I know you don't like to hear people call a lady a coon, but who is it?"

"I think it important," says Jackson, "to discuss and explore Stevens's misogyny and racism. To do so does not threaten to render him irrelevant or unworthy of his canonical place in American literature." In his reply, Vivek Narayanan suggested the dissonances a reader of color experiences, especially with the work of a racist—an author who never anticipated brown or Black fingers turning the pages of their books:

> as I read and enjoy and have my mind blown by Stevens, the identification can never be complete . . . I always read with the guess that there is no place for someone like me in the poems, that he would not even have conceived of a reader like me. In a way, it's thrilling to think of myself as an unintended reader, an interloper.
>
> Which again is not to say that I do not read and delight in and learn from Stevens' poetry on a daily basis—I do—but to say that one reads with a certain minor distance, a watchfulness, an alertness.

James Baldwin: "I was an interloper; this was not my heritage." I read Narayanan's comment with a spasm of recognition. Yes, I've always thought of myself as "an unintended reader, an interloper," beginning when, as a child, I plucked from my parents' shelves the works of white, canonical authors. Those were books that felt not mine twice over.

—

IN THE LEXINGTON HOUSE, bookcases hid behind sofas or in nooks. It was an education in how unbookish people felt about books: valuing them but not placing them front and center. Once again the interloper, I went up on footstools, knelt on hardwood floors, for a better look. Picking up novels and putting them down again. One day—it was raining dully, with silent flashes of lightning—my phone pulsed with an email from Radio 3 in the UK. Would I deliver a radio essay on a Philip Larkin poem of my choice? I leapt at this connection to England, saying yes right away.

Fearful during the pandemic, of never seeing my seventy-something parents again—furious, at people refusing vaccination—I returned to Philip Larkin's "Ambulances." Reading it at school, I'd been held up by one line in particular:

> Closed like confessionals, they thread
> Loud noons of cities, giving back
> None of the glances they absorb.
> Light glossy grey, arms on a plaque,
> They come to rest at any kerb:
> All streets in time are visited.
>
> Then children strewn on steps or road,
> Or women coming from the shops
> Past smells of different dinners, see
> A wild white face that overtops
> Red stretcher-blankets momently
> As it is carried in and stowed,

And sense the solving emptiness
That lies just under all we do,
And for a second get it whole,
So permanent and blank and true.

That's the first half of the poem. Our teacher presented Larkin to us as a cornerstone of modern English poetry, admirable for his craft. In response, my classmates and I laughed at his almost virtuosic ability to be miserable. We didn't discuss his racism, a topic one can't avoid today. His detractors point to the slurs in his letters; his defenders, to his love of jazz (in reviews for the *Telegraph*, he praises Billie Holiday). Often, when someone like me is asked to speak about such a writer, it's expected that we discuss race. I was determined to spotlight other things.

Yet, remembering my Leeds classroom—that colorless sunlight peculiar to the north of England pouring through the window, a beam of it intervening between my teacher, reading Larkin aloud, and me and my peers—I did say something about that "wild white face" the poem pivots around. Though I'm now a professor of literature at Harvard, those three words turn back time. I become again that unsure teenager awestruck by a literary world containing few faces like his own. The face I saw each morning in the mirror—white only between the eyebrows, where my mother applied before my bus to school a protective daub of *thiruneeru*, or holy ash.

Larkin wrote in the mid-sixties, with England already a racial multiculture—yet thought only of whites. Why is it that I tied myself in knots to defend him? Maybe, I reasoned (silently, in that classroom, retreating into myself), even I'd look "wild" and "white" with illness . . . But that isn't convincing. Larkin could certainly have written a poem straightforwardly about a white person being picked up by an ambulance; Hull, where he lived, was a monoculture at that time. But his poem aspires to universality. He says "*all* streets in time are visited," yet assumes the patient is Caucasian. This means that Larkin's view of England includes "different dinners" but not different complexions.

Seated in class, I wanted to put my hand up, but didn't. (Or, I probably did, but only to say something my teacher would reward, about the rhyme scheme.) I think a student of color would speak up, nowadays. They know how to articulate such disquiets. I didn't. That would take some time.

—

THE BOOKS OF SEMI-STRANGERS on the shelves in Lexington replaced, temporarily, those Jenny and I—both writers, and avid readers; writing and reading is like exhaling and inhaling, one process—had amassed down the years. She, a writer of fiction with a background in comparative literature, contributed Tolstoy, Alasdair Gray, Zola, Ferrante—books living alongside, in no particular order, my review copies of poetry, and dog-eared lit-crit: *Seven Types of Ambiguity*, *The Sense of an Ending* (the lectures of Frank Kermode, not the less creative Julian Barnes novel). Our books, and much else, had been separately shipped across the Atlantic and were now in a storage facility. I imagined vast, corrugated shipping containers, as in the second season of *The Wire*, and thousands of pages inside them slowly yellowing, the covers of paperbacks dissolving like rotting flesh. How many times had Jenny and I migrated from flat to flat within England, amazing movers with that sheer volume of books for which we always apologized, since they had to be toted in special, half-filled boxes, or become as impossibly heavy as dark matter—summoning what Seamus Heaney calls in one of his poems "a socket-ripping, / Life-belittling force— // Gravity's black box, the immovable / Stamp and squat and square-root of dead weight"? When I sent my first collection of poems to my mother as a Word document, she couldn't believe it was so small: she thought the file size should tally with the content.

Once your library swells, books from long ago may grow mysterious, auratic, as if someone else purchased them. I become an interloper, then, among my own possessions, trying to catch myself off guard, going back to novels, stories, poems, that once left me cold—wishing to discover I've changed. Sometimes I have. Sometimes, it's the same dog-eared pages, underlined sentences, and half-memorized stanzas that captivate.

—

OUR LAST EVENING IN CAMBRIDGE—the other Cambridge, in England, where I was a research fellow—we sat past sunset on the fire escape outside my flat, drinking white wine. My time there had expired. Another job application was rejected every week. Jenny worked across the street: you could see into her office from our bedroom window, and sometimes she snuck back at lunch to join me in bed. On the eve of our departure, she began to explain, slowly, struggling for words as the light failed, how a man at her workplace had harassed her for months. In person, and with email after email. Why hide this from me? "I didn't want you to worry, you're going through so much."

How much had been going on inside her? How violated she must have felt, returning day after day to that office. As dusk extinguished the fire escape, I felt ashamed. On I went, petitioning university after university for a job, and there was Jenny, turning up every day to another distressing email in her inbox, with its written voice that would not brook rejection. Another male voice that would never stop trying.

—

THE LEXINGTON BOOKSHELVES were filled with self-help. I flinched from it, remembering my mother's wish that I stop thinking and start living. Wasn't literature the real self-help? Only in America did I realize what millions have always known: that self-help provides (to repurpose Oscar Wilde's quip about cigarettes) "the perfect type of a perfect pleasure. It is exquisite, and it leaves one unsatisfied." A short-lived flare of feel-good enlightenment activates then fades. While reading, you feel as if—they're religious texts, really—you could with a snap of the fingers transform your life. But it never works: the high doesn't last.

The experience, repeated whenever you buy another—there were dozens in the Lexington house—develops into a rhythm. Highs and lows, peaks and troughs: many aspects of our culture could be discussed the same way. Shame, as I mentioned in my introduction, replaced only fleetingly and precariously with pride. I am reminded of, in popular music, the alternations of abjection and empowerment marketed to women. And of—returning to the genius of Gwendolyn Brooks—her novella, or extended prose poem, or collection of narratively interlinked prose poems, *Maud Martha*, where her heroine does consider "popular songs":

> "A popular song," thought she, "especially if it's one of the old, soft ones, is beautiful, sometimes, and seems to touch your mood exactly. But the touch is usually not full. You rise up with a popular song, but it isn't able to rise as high, once it has you started, as you are; by the time you've risen as high as it can take you you can't bear to stop, and you swell up and up and up till you're swelled to bursting. The popular music has long ago given up and left you."

Maud Martha is a poor Black woman in the mid-twentieth-century US; Brooks's lyrical prose considers the limits of lyricism. Some types of uplift are untrue; since Brooks is acidulous about the disrespect shown to women like Martha by the men in her life—injured by white society, they take it out on women preferred pale not dark—the idea of music causing Maud Martha to swell as if pregnant, before giving up and leaving her, rather like a philandering male, has an edge to it.

—

THERE WAS A SCATTERING of poetry on the Lexington bookshelves: Sharon Olds, Wendell Berry, Mary Oliver. Poets breaking through to the mainstream reader. One Olds poem I reread whenever we gave Frank his bath. After gently washing his hair and his chubby arms and legs and belly, which, resembling a dolphin's back, glistened where it broke the churning surface, we'd sit back and watch as—supine and tenaciously, his black hair floating out from his face like, now, the gill stalks of an axolotl—Frank kicked and kicked with his legs as if swimming. His total absorption and self-involved joy and unfettered experimentation with the mysterious medium of water felt like a reproach. Unlike him, neither Jenny nor I could stay within the present moment. There was always too much possible doom to ruminate over, or a fantasized future into which to retreat. So keeping one eye on Frank, Jenny took out her phone. And I returned to Olds's "The Sign of Saturn."

The allusion is to the god devouring his own children (as in Goya's painting, where his teeth tear, as at jerky, at an already headless corpse). Olds's daughter, when angry, reminds the poet of her own father. Her sour look recalls the man passed out on the couch. "Sometimes I hear her talking to her brother / with that coldness that passed for reason in him," and,

> As I talk to her,
> trying to persuade her toward the human, her little
> clear face tilts as if she can
> not hear me, as if she were listening
> to the blood in her own ear, instead,
> her grandfather's voice.

None of us—Jenny, me, Frank with his developmental delays—seemed in those pandemic days, months, years, to really, clearly, hear each other. Isolation was somehow deafening, as if the mental noise of it, and the news, drowned out the conversations we sought to have as well as the words Frank struggled to shape—his tongue and mouth-muscles miswired. When our parents video-called, they turned out to share across schisms of culture and race identical old-person struggles with webcams pointed the wrong way, smudged lenses, voices accidentally muted, malfunctioning routers. The fantasy we shared at the beginning of lockdown, of technology fulfilling all our needs! Before faces onscreen began to glitch, like the androids on *Westworld* going awry. The Capgras delusion: Was this person shrunk down, as if living inside my phone, and gesturing with intensity, like someone drowning in a sea of unreliable pixels—with gaps of freeze to their talk, as if time stopped and restarted—was she really the woman who gave birth to me?

How exhausting it was: the labor of pretending from day to day that everything was fine—for the sake of our parents, and Frank. We were terrified of his malleability, of his first years determining the rest of his life: as if, should pandemic reality seep through our defenses into his very bones, there would be no recovering from it. Unknowingly, I acted like my parents, shielding my child from trauma through exaggerated performances of positivity, the sort of willed happiness common to immigrants and impossible to sustain.

Often, fighting, Jenny and I did accuse each other of repeating our parents. I said she was cold, uneffusive, looming at me then withdrawing. For her part, Jenny observed how capriciously impulsive I was, like all Ravinthirans: a family operating forever in crisis-mode, whose psychic highs and lows had (like those of popular music) untied themselves from the actual peaks and troughs of life.

As for Frank—and Olds's poem—whose voice was he tuned into, staring into space with those big, glistening eyes? Sometimes, bouncing him in my arms, I began to confess to Frank—since he couldn't respond—my worst worries. His radiant, becalmed gaze made him a little Buddha. Like those statues we noticed in house after house in the North-East of England, in the former pit-villages we visited to retrieve secondhand furniture purchased through Facebook, from people who had found, in the aftermath of Margaret Thatcher's depredations, desire to indeed be, as Siddhartha Gautama put it, inextricable from suffering.

Frank didn't yet exist, occupy a space within, our world of turbulent self-concern. It was in our gift to induct him.

—

MY FATHER WAS BEATEN (I don't mean, *defeated*) by his father. Now he rages at sloppy motorists, dilatory waiters, any rule-breaker. He'll never target me, my sister, or my mother: it is possible to observe him converting his frustration, say, with my slowness to get dressed and leave the house, into road rage or reactionary blurts about politics. Unlike his wife, he has devised a crisp, unembarrassable English accent and a well-groomed gravitas amplified, even, during the years when his vitiligo worsened, to the point of his skin turning white. Not the white of white people's skin, with its patches of pink and yellow, striations and wrinkles and moles, and the micronetworks of burst capillaries that, when I began in my teens to really notice the people around me, became a source of wonder. My father's skin when it turned white (his forehead and hairline, for instance, where his black hair-dye aggravated the condition) was bone-white—as if the skin had disappeared entirely, leaving only a gleam of skull. He was white as ancient Greek sculpture is white, its paint having rubbed off over eons, creating icons of apparently purified, abstract beauty out of originally vibrant, eye-startling beings meant, like the gods of painted concrete in a Hindu temple, to, even coarsely, grab one's attention.

It became easier to paint pale, with makeup, the remaining patches of brown. Traveling in Sri Lanka, he was mistaken for white: my father's curated accent and skin condition merged into an expressive performance chosen as a destiny rather than suffered as an affliction. Eventually he ordered a special heat lamp and grew gently browner, with a polynesia of recrudescent coffee-color branding one cheek—resuming the complexion that was his birthright.

When he arrived in Yorkshire, patients asked for another, a white, doctor. Does the anger come of his painful childhood in Batticaloa, or his experiences in 1970s England? My father has shrunk himself down, determined not to offend. His accent and his appearance have adjusted to negate, not answer, the question: "Who's that paki?"

—

WAS IT MY FATHER'S STATUS as a doctor that intensified my encounter with Larkin's "Ambulances" at school? "Ambulances" takes seriously the idea, sneered at by the Conservative politician Nigel Lawson (whom I quote with disrelish), that the National Health Service "is the closest thing the English people have to a religion." Founded by Aneurin Bevan in 1948, the NHS and its ambulances link communities. Moving from street to street, these vehicles perform a ritual giving collective meaning to otherwise isolated suffering. That's why Larkin compares them to Catholic "confessionals." Ambulances in transit suture locales as with a needle and "thread"—imagining a doctor stitching a wound, let's remember the derivation of religion, from the Latin *religio*, "to bind together." Larkin was, famously, an atheist. But this poem wants to believe in something. Reading it aloud, so its meter, rhyme, and syntax become ceremonious, I remember the prayer my mother muttered under her breath as she applied that holy ash to my forehead.

Larkin's most spiritually despairing poem—"Aubade," scanting religion as "That vast moth-eaten musical brocade / Created to pretend we never die"—ends with "postmen" who "like doctors go from house to house." Another ritual. A further poem, "Days," mentions "the priest and the doctor / In their long coats / Running over the fields." "Ambulances" considers the National Health Service a substitute for the Church. But city ambulances don't, like rural doctors or priests, "go from house to house" on rounds. They sprint to emergencies: when Larkin says of those vehicles that they "come to rest" at any curb, this doesn't feel right. He's really thinking about people, dying; of, perhaps, Shakespeare's *Cymbeline*: "Golden lads and girls all must, / As chimney-sweepers, come to dust."

Writing my radio essay, I paused to consider the deep snow in our borrowed backyard, sparkling in the New England sunlight and marked only by a rabbit's bluish prints, and the tinier tracks left by a bird. Separated from family in the UK, I felt especially protective of the NHS (viciously attacked by Republicans, when Obama tried to institute universal healthcare in the US). In this context, Larkin's poem about how we're each isolated within ourselves, like a person enclosed by an ambulance, touched me deeply, and I was drawn to what seemed praise of the NHS, since in Massachusetts we'd no choice but to accept the private insurance offered by my employer, with its dizzying fine print listing exclusions and co-pays.

I remembered from my childhood in Leeds one ambulance in particular, coming for my father—he'd had a heart attack. He wouldn't stop playing doctor, even as the patient, but decided to phone 999 without waking, and worrying, me. My mother returned from work and went in the ambulance with him. I was left behind in the empty house, to pick up the shopping strewn across the floor—those heavy bags that had overstrained his heart.

Ambulances are modernity's harbingers of disaster, messengers from the gods, arriving the way a bad omen or a clap of thunder might once have done. They are reminders, perhaps, that the world is a dangerous place, that good health isn't guaranteed, that we've forgotten to count our blessings. Taking my first steps into fatherhood, finding my way and in a country not my own, I began to wonder about the beliefs, morals, I would pass on to my son. My upbringing left me with a faith in medicine and also, though my parents never went to temple and were only intermittently practicing Hindus, a sense of fate, even fatalism. Being Sri Lankan Tamils, subjugated back home and also as immigrants to England, my mother and father raised me to consider the world a dangerous place leaving one in need of protection, divine or otherwise. Even now, their heightened sense of fragility and peril had them worry about the icy conditions of

New England, and whether I—or Jenny, or Frank—would trip and fall.

In "Ambulances," Larkin's spectators—women and children—"sense the solving emptiness / That lies just under all we do." They feel alone with the thought of their own inevitable death. Why women and children? It's as if Larkin were describing a war-situation, from which women and children were traditionally excluded: we should consider the proximity of World War II to the founding of the NHS.

As the ambulance departs, the existential crisis it provoked turns out to be temporary. Here's the second half of the poem:

> The fastened doors recede. Poor soul,
> They whisper at their own distress;
>
> For borne away in deadened air
> May go the sudden shut of loss
> Round something nearly at an end,
> And what cohered in it across
> The years, the unique random blend
> Of families and fashions, there
>
> At last begin to loosen. Far
> From the exchange of love to lie
> Unreachable inside a room
> The traffic parts to let go by
> Brings closer what is left to come,
> And dulls to distance all we are.

It seems "they," those watching the ambulance, evade its

grim truth with an empty phrase: "Poor soul." They commiserate tokenistically, pushing the issue and the person heading to hospital out of mind. Another ritual. Is Larkin being cynical about the onlookers, saying they're interested only in themselves? I think he's more tender than that—the situation is complex.

Again, I consider my father. When I'm with him and an ambulance flashes by, he always says the same thing. Not "poor soul," but "I hope they make it." Seeing an ambulance, we don't know who's inside, and this anonymity, though it sets limits to fellow feeling, also makes it possible. Imagine if we lived in Facebook's "metaverse" in which, as the ambulance went by, our augmented brains got a real-time readout about the person within. We might learn unpleasant things about them, details with which to thrust their pain aside, saying (instead of "poor soul") "he deserves it." In the real world, as in Larkin's poem, it's the very absence of knowledge about the ambulance's occupant that ensures them a place in our feelings, though it also means they can become a stand-in for ourselves.

I used to feel cynical about public outpourings of grief following the death of celebrities—crowds of strangers lining the streets, the flowers and messages. But as the psychoanalyst Darian Leader explains, it is the role of collective mourning to allow the public to access and express their own, multifarious, griefs, linked to events that may have occurred years ago. Larkin walks the line, between criticizing people for behaving this way—seeing the ambulance, and grieving really for themselves—and accepting that it couldn't be otherwise.

By the poem's end, the ambulance meant to save lives

becomes a tomb. The silence of the grave replaces that of the confessional. A sinuous syntax takes us from outside the vehicle to within, suddenly, the failing consciousness inside. Earlier, Larkin suggested that onlookers couldn't feel for that person. Now he shows it is possible to feel as if it were you, or me, being taken away: an act of imaginative teleportation "dulls to distance all we are." As so often in Larkin's poems, a grandiose final claim is made, a claim to which we needn't assent. (Seeing an ambulance go by, I don't feel annihilated, "dulled to distance"—how about you?) But a poem, like a person, can be admired without our agreeing with it.

I side not with the Larkin phobic of otherness but with the poet entrusting himself to the National Health Service. During the pandemic, many seemed, to borrow Larkin's word, "unreachable" in a new way—imprisoned within echo chambers of misinformation—I was heartened by this poem's emphasis on interdependence.

Inspired by Larkin's poem, I decided to video-call my parents as often as I could bear, following Frank around with the camera as he raced this way and that. And when my mother began, mysteriously, to convert her rage at the mishandling of the crisis into what appeared a Stockholm syndrome sufferer's inexplicable attachment, to the Conservative Party ("our Boris," is how she referred to the ailing PM), I didn't argue, but changed the subject. Sometimes I teased her about my childhood: all the Hindu prayers, the holy ash. Did she feel the *thiruneeru* was necessary, a daily inoculation for her son against the dangers of white England? Or was it an expression of both togetherness and gratitude?

—

THERE IS ANXIETY in my family (Jenny suggested I title this book *The Influence of Anxiety*, as a jab at Harold Bloom), but also an undercurrent of rage. As Olds recognizes, furies are transmitted down the generations. My sister, ten years older than me, put on as a teenager my father's tempestuousness with his name and his complexion—his gender wasn't required. She terrified me. My fights with the parents were obscurer, and worth investigating here (I might learn something).

My sister's rebellion resembled those films in which the East clashes with the West, and Western values win—she wished to work in a pub, wear ripped jeans, and defeated my parents in their stereotypical aim of making doctors of us. As a result, I didn't fight that fight: but children and parents *must* fight. So another confrontation was engineered, concerning the orange-robed holy man Sai Baba, photographs of whom my parents framed on the walls. One day I insisted they take them down. I wanted him—in Twitter parlance—canceled. I'd found evidence online that he was a fraud (he used to "materialize" watches for his devotees, hiding them up his flame-colored silk sleeves) and a pedophile. My mother protested. In Sri Lanka, shrines to Sai Baba—framed photographs of his broad, beige, complacent face; the nonplussing afro-like hair, once black, eventually gray—were the site of miracles. Even if covered by glass, *thiruneeru* appeared on the images overnight, in beautiful patterns no human hand could create.

But it's not true, I cried. Your beliefs are false. This man isn't holy, and there is no God.

"As if she can / not hear me," writes Olds. "Can / not," where the line-break may stand for the division between mother and daughter, isn't the same as "cannot." Olds is disturbed by the possibility that a child may really not hear her mother, that she possesses a power of inattentiveness opposite to how things should biologically be.

Often, our tiny clan of three, struggling to outlast the pandemic, seemed ready to crumble. I looked across at Frank nestled in my wife's arms, and felt isolated not only from friends and family thousands of miles away, and from the colleagues and students whose digital companionship it was terrible to lose at the end of a semester, but also from the two people trapped with me in a house that wasn't ours.

—

ONCE, WAKING IN THE OLIVE-GREEN guest room—we'd agreed not to touch the master suite—I forgot where in the world I was. Place and time were abolished. My wife's shape in the darkness; the screen of the baby monitor, where Frank lay in his white sleep-bag, glowing like the Milky Way: these weren't landmarks. I felt untethered, maybe happily so—unhistorical, guilt-free, streamlined. What had happened, and what might yet, ceased to occupy any mental space. The bulk of brooding being melted into nothing. Turning the handle of the bathroom door the wrong way the first time, I came up against my face in the mirror, among a galaxy of toothpaste-speckles, and thought of robots, and clones. Who was I, really? What had I become? Seeing suddenly (I had shaved my beard off, for the first time in years) how my face had aged.

When we drove to CVS to have our photographs taken for our green card applications, the website—its racially illiberal algorithm—would not accept the storeworker's attempts to capture my face. Jenny and Frank, their photos done, had to wait while she tried over and over. No, my head did not take up more than 69 percent of the image's total height; the background had not, due to cloud-shadow or a glitch in the store's soft lighting, changed to a shade undefinable as either white or off-white; yes, I directly faced the camera, in all six—so far—rejected attempts, trying my best to evince a neutral expression (not my growing despair). Was it my beard, obscuring the lower half of my face, and its tusks of silver hair seeming to descend from either side of my mouth? Or the squint in my left eye, that, ever since, as a child, I crashed into a radiator, has never opened fully?

My face was not an American face. The computer would not accept it.

—

ALTHOUGH JENNY AND I eventually bought our own house, and unpacked our books, we are still unpacking our experience of the pandemic and coming to terms with its lingering effects. Not for the first time am I reminded, by events in my own life, of things in Sri Lanka. Going through a grievance process at an old job, I was struck by the resemblance of Human Resources rhetoric—"let's not look back, but try to move on"—to the attitudes of the Sri Lankan government and some of its people, to the civil war. Gordon Weiss, formerly UN ambassador there, gives his perspective on the refusal of the government to look into the crime and corruption of the war—the countless missing, presumed dead, and innocents fired on with heavy weapons. He observes that in the West, it's assumed that countries acknowledge their histories (Germany, for instance, with its Holocaust memorials), but this view doesn't obtain in Sri Lanka. In fact, he's being idealistic, for the amnesia of Western nations concerning the inseparability of colonialism, empire, and immigration manifests a system of denials. But these nations do acknowledge at least some of the injustices that shaped them.

How rapidly we in the UK and the US have moved on from the pandemic, returning, as if self-protectively, to the same old grievances. Sometimes I sense in myself, even in the silent tension of the muscles around the corners of my eyes and my mouth, when I glance in the mirror before hurrying to work, something ever-imminent, a great scream of pain and frustration never vented, because the expressive forms for it haven't been discovered (very little television and film, it seems to me, gets to the heart of the pandemic experience). We cannot deny such things forever.

I remember traveling in Sri Lanka with my father, and pausing one day by the side of the road to consider a pile of stones. They had no markings, and my mind that is always bouncing between unlike things, as if making impulsive flights across the globe, turned to Ian Hamilton's "Memorial":

> Four weathered gravestones tilt against the wall
> Of your Victorian asylum.
> Out of bounds, you kneel in the long grass
> Deciphering obliterated names:
> Old lunatics who died here.

Gravestones weathered into illegibility: it's a short poem about, as Michael Hofmann notices, reading and attention; about getting frustrated with someone for paying attention not to us but, instead, to something bizarre and "out of bounds," in a distracted and even crazy way. They're just "old lunatics," the poem's speaker sneers—who cares? Don't cast yourself in with that lot. Come over here and talk to me instead.

But there's something curiously alive about those markers for the dead. They "tilt," they aren't "tilted"—an active verb, "tilt," like "you kneel," returns me to Olds's description of a child heeding not the wrong writing, in this case, but the wrong voice: "her little / clear face tilts as if she can / not hear me, as if she were listening to the blood in her own ear."

Those grass-overgrown, more than tilted, in fact erratically strewn, stones, were once markers in an LTTE graveyard. They commemorated deaths for the separatist cause—in some cases, people who blew themselves up, killing their enemies and uninvolved civilians. Tamil scholar Tho Paramasivan:

> Today, the Tamil word *arai* which means a room denotes a small living space for an individual. The word *kallarai* for a grave is just an extension of the word *arai*—*kal* + arai or stone room.
>
> . . . Scholars divide the burial grounds found in Tamilnadu into four categories. The first method is to place a stone or heap of stones on top of where the corpse was buried. Another involved placing a stone on top of the burial site and surrounding it with stones buried circularly around it up to a diameter of about fifteen feet. The

> third method was planting haphazardly sculpted rocks conically to a height of eight to ten feet on top of the burial site. The fourth method . . . resembles a room similar to the booths built for security guards at the entrance of large buildings we see today.
>
> . . . The word *kallarai* was probably born out of this practice of building a room-like structure with stones for the dead.
>
> . . . The putting up of such graveyard structures preceded the birth of Christ, say archaeologists. A small word tells the story of humanity ever so subtly. Tamil has many such words.

The Sri Lankan army razed Tamil graveyards, seeing them as terrorist sites. My parents, choosing not to teach their children Tamil, wished to draw a line under their past. I thought this a generational thing—an inability to glimpse the richness of a bilingual inheritance—until I spoke with my cousin Prem, who moved to Sydney with his wife and two children. He'd no plan to teach them Tamil either. "We live in Australia now," he said.

But someone—I wonder who; a person both intent and distracted, like the addressee of Hamilton's poem—regathered in that bleak place the smashed gravestones into a cairn. People refuse to forget—even the horror of a son or daughter donning an explosive vest.

# *To be Frank*

Jones Tavern is one of the oldest buildings in our town of Acton, Massachusetts—built in 1732, segmentally extended, and gutted by fire in the 1960s, its walls and beams and doors keep that black, scaly look in the bar downstairs. We took Frank when he was three. Patiently from room to room he roamed, scrutinizing dates on posters—he loves letters and numbers—and sprinting through a rope-cordoned door, so I had to pull him back and explain (though I couldn't work out the reasoning myself) you were meant to enter from the other side. He noticed all the modern technology—embarrassing our guide, by pointing at smoke alarms, cables, power switches: "You'll have to imagine those things aren't here," she said.

This interaction fascinated me, perhaps because, in New England, we've been surprised, as English people, that historical buildings and new ones constructed to look like them are hard to tell apart. In *old* England, it's thought naff—unless you're King Charles in Poundbury—to build houses in antiquated styles. In Acton, there isn't so much *visual* difference from the outside, between Jones Tavern and our own clapboard house in the, a word I can never hear or say unselfconsciously, *colonial* style. Pastiche is not considered tasteless here. Or, as you might put it, masking.

—

IT FELT AS IF OUR SON, born in the Midlands prior to his transplantation to the East Coast, was making a point, about the tenuousness of ideas of authenticity, by spotlighting (it must have felt like this, to our guide) odds and ends of modern wiring. Upstairs, he came alive, noticing a rug and a table on it both the shape of his favorite number—zero. "Oval" was a word recently learned: he used to say "dear-dear shushle"—that is, a circle deformed by some unspecified trauma.

Frank inspired me to write this book as I have done, seeking to understand my life through encounters with poems that, on the face of it, are about very different things. He is my example from day to day of how the world can be gradually understood through a process of analogy: restlessly, he compares one object with another.

—

FRANK IS FASCINATED by everything that isn't quite as it should be, that is damaged or has begun to malfunction; which applies to the people in his life too—his focus, to quote the Italian poet Valerio Magrelli (in Jamie McKendrick's translation), is whatever betrays "the unmistakable / whirr and clunk / of the bust contraption," wherever "a bit sticks out, / breaks off, declares itself." The crossing light outside Jones Tavern was inactive for months. "Dear-*dear* light," said Frank, still—otherwise—speech-delayed.

I, much worried over by my parents, and marinating within a culture of worrying, tell my son every day that it's okay for things to change, often unpredictably.

"He's a pandemic child," they say. "He's one of the coronavirus babies. We just don't know how it has affected them."

—

FRANK SPRANG INTO ACTION, inspired by the zero-resembling rug, and table, and the thought-feeling of the words "zero" and "oval" arriving in his head. He made instantaneously a nourishing sort of sense out of that otherwise alien building. Finding a lifeline, but also more than that; he was abruptly, absolutely, happy, like me when a poem (that I'm reading, or writing) begins to resolve in my mind, and the resistances of language are replaced by, nothing passively compliant, but a feeling of furtherance nevertheless, a matching of its opacities with my own.

Imagine a conversation at the corner of the room, between two wallflowers otherwise miserable at a party whose vibe never sat right with them, and into whose element they had longed, individually, to plunge, but without success, until, finally, this fortuitous encounter.

—

FRANK ONCE PERCEIVED the world like a cubist painter, in terms of the few shape-words he could manage; a *pole*, to him, could be a snow pole, a strand of spaghetti, a cat's whisker, the wire charging our tablet, or one of my, or his mother's, rapidly increasing number of gray hairs ("dear-dear shair"). Most of us consider poles *hard* things: Frank was decidedly unphallogocentric. In Jones Tavern he ran to open and close an old, warped door, rushing between a bedroom and the sagging steps of the landing. Frank liked this enclosed and manipulable space. He felt freed and so did we, watching him.

—

OUR GUIDE STOOD in the doorframe, so Frank couldn't open and close it as he wished.

I have written that sentence as if she did it on *purpose*. Why is this?

Is it because after we left Jones Tavern, we saw a car decorated with Trump stickers, and wondered was it hers? I may have turned her, that is, into someone to be angry with, and, worse, to *resent*; to be with Frank is frequently to feel as if one *were* Frank, with his odd and, to strangers, inexplicable habits. It is difficult to be consistently misunderstood without becoming defensive.

Not for Frank. He didn't fight back, and doesn't blame the guide for what happened. If he remembered the incident (he doesn't), it would be without resentment, though it was due to her that he sank to his knees, and sobbed, and wailed—

—

FRANK WAS DIAGNOSED with autism spectrum disorder when he was two and a half, at the beginning of 2022.

The poet and editor and mentor without whom I wouldn't be writing this now—he edited my first chapbook of poems—came to his diagnosis too late. Roddy Lumsden, a Scot who moved to London, shaping the UK poetry scene creatively and as, in particular, a supporter of women and writers of color, was, though with hundreds of friends, one of the loneliest people I've ever met. Roddy self-medicated with alcohol, and died of it. He published "Autism" in Prac Crit, a magazine I co-edited, in 2015:

> Some nights I catch the smell
>         of the lives of others,
> all that is awry, agley,
>         the washers loose,
> the springs rust-bunged.
>         Or the sheerest glee
> I hope and fear that friends may feel:
>         their refound wallet
> or the cat returned after a week
>         and just a little thin.
> And when I say I smell this, I am
>         talking creosote,
> broth smog, thinners. The room hangs
>         round the smell,
> would bow to its bidding or bawl
>         at its funeral.
> I strain to enter the life of another,
>         to bathe them, taunt them,
> treat. For people mainly think they only
>         think they think that
> no one thinks like them. But I too

have met against
your tarriest thought, your sick ambition,
lay late with a knife
in my mind, or a pulse of appalling glory.
We are alike as mercury
and nickel are, as leopard and gazelle
might blink in unison.
Even my siblings are disarmingly other.
And as a man walking
through all hours of darkness, clearing
to clearing, stile to well
to glebe to turnpike, I catch a gamey taint
of other beings, softly
being, grinding in foliage, cowering in boles,
zedding to warrens.
Paralleling you in bed, I give marginally less
of myself when sleep
grips its pliers. No one has ever known me.
Is that cute? I hear a woman
say, 'I died that night.' A man in the audience
shouts out in the quiet part
of the play. Some self-styled prophet screams,
full minute, on the beach
and all the poppets scatter from the sea,
gapey-eyed and clinging
at Mummy. I count these sifting colours
of my brief spectrum,
halfwise touching each in turn. You should
believe me when I say
that what I am seeing now is something
you must never see.

—

RODDY DIED IN 2020, aged just fifty-three.

Many autistic people understand their worldview as not deficient but *different*: they are "disabled" only in that society is constructed with neurotypical people in mind. (There are also people requiring greater accommodations, who, along with their carers, consider the older idea of disability a must.) I am all for—thinking of Frank, as always, and racing to return to him, along his curve of thought—such empowerment. But I also love Roddy's poem for its unreconciled alienation, for how its incessant inventiveness records a harangued mind's sauntering between experiences of humiliation and compensatory grandiosity; recording, but also critiquing, how those who've suffered for being different learn to cling to and revalue that difference as uniqueness—a gesture becoming rigid, snobby, when we claim our difference makes us *better* than others. Such is the "pulse of appalling glory" Roddy mentions. He's tempted by it, but turns back. "No one has ever known me," he announces, but again self-subverts: "Is that cute?" As he explains to Kathryn Maris,

> It's a way of undercutting the rather preposterous preceding line, "No one has ever known me." There is a part of me that absolutely means that "no one has ever known me"—but at the same time it's a little bit of a lofty thing to say. Or maybe not lofty, but it's a bit of a big, melodramatic statement. No one has ever known me! I wanted to undercut that; I was being a bit hammy.

One of the best things poetry can do for us, is incorporate, aerate, explore, such mixed and shifting thoughts. It can expose self-pity as a coping mechanism while revealing alternative, less domineering, ways of being kind to ourselves about aspects of our personalities unshareable with others, no matter how hard we, or they, try to connect. As Roddy puts it:

> I worry that I will get other people wrong. And I think there's a bit in the poem where I say even my siblings I sometimes find hard to gauge. So even the people very, very close to you—you can sometimes get them wrong. And perhaps we all get people wrong, but I think those of us with spectrum conditions are very prone to getting people wrong, and you have to spend your whole life teaching yourself to get people right. I've written so much about miscommunication, simply because I have such a fear of miscommunicating.

—

PREVENTED FROM OPENING and closing a three-hundred-year-old door, Frank couldn't do what he needed. He experienced an obstruction (the opening and closing of doors is his experience of making an obstruction appear and disappear at will). I should have asked our guide to allow Frank to resume his game, his zone, his unique approach to the strangeness of that building.

I think about this incident often—crushed by guilt.

—

RODDY'S POEM, LIKE FRANK, is curious about "all that is awry, agley": muddling with the machinic a lexis of élan vital, he pictures people as creaturely automatons. Everyone, although there is a predator class (the neurotypical) and its prey (autistic people). It's also about, however, being a Scot in London, another kind of outsider, since "agley" alludes to Robert Burns's famous poem "To a Mouse."

Burns's epigraph tells us the speaker of the poem has, in November 1785, turned "her up in her Nest, with the Plough." He is male and the mouse is female (a "wee, sleeket, cowran, tim'rous beastie"): we could read it as an apology poem from a man to a startled, put-upon, even harassed, woman, and Roddy's response-poem is ambivalent about his own possibly creepy sexuality. He is an autistic man who struggles to articulate his desires and feels shunned and feared. But Burns is also writing about the damage we do to nature and other living beings. "I'm truly sorry Man's dominion / Has broken Nature's social union":

> But Mousie, thou art no thy-lane,
> In proving foresight may be vain:
> The best laid schemes o' Mice an' Men
> Gang aft agley,
> An' lea'e us nought but grief an' pain,
> For promis'd joy!

The poet tries to break down the barrier between himself and the mouse: she's not alone, he says ("no thy-lane"), in living precariously. He expresses this sentiment in lines that have become idiomatic.

With one word, Roddy activates our memory of this

poem and its central sentiment, summoning its power-dynamic but also its communalism. He challenges a restrictive idea of the human (the bigoted idea that some are more human than others). He sees us as animals "zedding to warrens": does this mean, creatures running in shapes like *Z*s; or that they're heading home to sleep, to catch some z's? Both meanings are in the dictionary: it might seem Roddy has invented this word, that it's a neologism, but he has actually salvaged something discarded (as a person can be discarded, ostracized). His autistic poetics investigates relentlessly the relation between sound and sense. Can sound become a new *kind* of sense?

"I hear a woman / say, 'I died that night.'" This is the sort of metaphor autistic people are meant to misunderstand. In the sort of patronizing anecdote told about them—Remi Yergeau, in *Authoring Autism*, observes biases clouding even scientific materials—we read of autistic people stymied by figurative situations, like Roddy's "man in the audience" who "shouts out in the quiet part / of the play" (he could also be someone who cannot control his vocalizations). But this view of autistic languaging as overly literal is outdated. As Julia Miele Rodas tells us, that which "is frequently understood as rigid and mechanical" is actually "profoundly elastic and creative." When Frank wanted me to zip up my hoodie over my blue T-shirt, he used to say "boo night-night": *put the blue T-shirt to sleep*. Observing a rabbit eating clover, he said, "no shar" (it isn't sitting on a chair, as he would, as his mother and father do, when eating). When I compare how Frank speaks now—eloquently by any standard, though with a distinctive prosody—to the miracles he managed while speech-delayed, I think of Oulipo writers, doing extraordinary things with a restricted vocabulary. Jenny's brother became "dear-dear Mummy" because he resembled her but imperfectly (in his appearance, as well as his displays of affection?); baked beans, a British staple now expensively imported (Boston beans are *very* different), were "red dear-dear shushles."

Roddy was an expert with trivia machines and his poems resemble assemblages from a factoid-hoard that is also a word-hoard. Marvelous sound-shapes coalesce, collide, seeming both connected and not—spooky action at a distance. He liked lists and refrains and to test a word's taste by placing it unexpectedly in a verse-line. Ralph Savarese: "Pattern . . . is what attracts classical autistics to poetry." Roddy generated new patterns, forms, rules, delighting in naming and sharing them with others: he was an inspiring teacher, mentor, editor, and friend. How point-blankly, I remember, he once called out a racist on Facebook: "Racist." How badly he coped with the pernicious false manners of the poetry world, convincing himself a certain king and queen maker, a powerful editor, must like him after all, because at a do she deigned to kiss him on the cheek.

—

ONE OF THE WORST ableist myths about autistic people is that they're uninterested in other people. "I strain to enter the life of another," writes Roddy, activating this idea, before complicating things: "to bathe it, taunt it, treat." "Strain" is an active verb. He says simultaneously that he struggles to leap the gap between himself and another being, and that he's trying his best. Bathe, taunt, treat: these words suggest neurotypical exchanges, mingling kindness and banter, gift-giving and gift-receiving, an ebb and flow of signals the autistic person can't master.

Roddy knows he's working with a neurotypical reader's received ideas about what autism is. And he also knows that contemporary multicultures trouble that ideal of the sympathetic imagination exalted by the Romantic poet Percy Bysshe Shelley, in his "Defence of Poetry":

> The great secret of morals is Love; or a going out of our own nature, and an identification of ourselves with the beautiful which exists in thought, action, or person, not our own. A man to be greatly good must imagine intensely and comprehensively; he must put himself in the place of another and of many others; the pains and pleasures of his species must become his own.

What does difference do with difference? Meeting someone who isn't me, do I try to enter their minds, or would that be violation, appropriation, conquest? Do I identify with the other person, or accept the impossibility of doing so as a precondition of respect? Issues of race, class, gender, nationality, of power and privilege, feverishly foreground these questions.

—

CULTURAL REPRESENTATIONS often have little to do with actual autistic people. We assume, for one thing, that they're men, and are only slowly realizing that many women, like my wife, learned in childhood to—at great cost—mask behaviors unsettling to others, living for decades without the diagnosis that would transform their life. But it is for Jenny to write about this, in her fiction, in her brilliant and inimitable way. Let me discuss, instead—as a, by present definitions, neurotypical, if deeply odd, member of an "autism family"—problems of race. For it's a *white man* we see in our minds, when we think of autism—playing a particular role in the imagination of a culture. There he is—slender, discomposed, spiky, overassertive. I am supposed to both laugh at and admire him for how he always does the same thing and reacts in the same way and has no time for others. He is, as E. M. Forster remarked of the novels of Dickens, a *flat character*.

He looks nothing like Frank. He doesn't even remind me of Roddy.

A racialized critique of cultural representations of autism might begin with the televisual omnipresence of this white man; and go on to consider the appropriation of autism, to our need to go on praising and validating styles of white masculinity otherwise outdated—by treating them ironically, tempering our love with laughter; by activating autism as an excuse for this white man's self-centeredness as the price one must pay (that we *love* to pay) in exchange for his extraordinary powers. For he is also, always, the cleverest person in the room.

—

WE OPERATE WITH RIGID HIERARCHIES of privilege, and a narrowed, defiantly unambiguous, sense of who is the victim and who the aggressor in any given situation. It's worth considering the challenge of autism to this social politics.

If many autistic people identify as cis men, and are white, isn't there a danger of people like me misinterpreting behavior that is ultimately innocuous, and to do with neurodivergence, as hostile?

An example. Frank was for a while obsessed with trees. I installed an app on my phone to identify the unfamiliar flora and fauna of New England, and took him to the arboretum. He loved, especially, running up and poking the bark, giggling—tryouts, it could be, for interacting with people. He perceived something vaguely scandalous about invading, as it were, a tree's personal space. It became a family joke.

One day, we were crossing and perhaps recrossing a wooden footpath (Frank likes these too, anything resembling a bridge), when a boy of ten or so appeared with his mother, and began explaining to Frank that one of the trees was in fact two trees that had grown so close to each other that they had merged. You could discern, he pointed out, the two kinds of bark. We have always appreciated the interest of other, often older, children in Frank, and listened with pleasure. Then, as the mother and son walked away, she turned to look over her shoulder at us, apologetically.

Was that boy autistic? At what point do we stop telling our often "wee, sleeket, cowran, tim'rous" autistic children to advocate for themselves, and instead to stop urging their special interests on others? Apprehending others neurodiversely (in time, the category of "neurotypical" may itself prove unsatisfactory) may require giving them the benefit of the doubt, *prior* to the imposition of labels. From an autistic perspective, overexplaining (performed by a person of any gender) reappears not as a quest for domination but as a well-intentioned try at connection, and perhaps at regulating (not dominating) an interaction otherwise overwhelming.

I'm concerned about rage-circuits, cause-and-effect narratives of grievance and blame, that—though I might agree, with the politics behind them—have begun to overwrite, flatten, and marginalize forms of being slipping through the cracks of our increasingly vicious conversations around power and pain, aggression and victimhood. We are relational beings: it isn't easy to separate behavior that hurts others from uncontrollable quirks of the personality, although to listen in on arguments online is often to witness an increasingly desperate desire to do just that. "He's just an asshole. I'm autistic too, and I would never do such a thing . . . "

In a low-tolerance culture, where it has become harder and harder not to leap to defensiveness, the power of a clinical diagnosis to radically shift our perspective on others becomes unhealthily exaggerated. If it's possible for us to move, in a given encounter, from feeling harassed and subjugated, to—when realizing the other person is autistic, or of another disenfranchised subject position—reevaluating that behavior in a kinder light, we might also consider "neurotypical," like "AAPI" or "BAME," a provisional statistext: a bureaucratic category. From one perspective, no one is typical, and the dividing line between consciously willed and involuntary behavior toward others can be faint. Supporting those who've suffered, we may also understand those who *cause* pain as, sometimes, far from malign.

I hope that our future understandings of neurodiversity would have us consider each other kindly (questioning, also, the pleasures of righteousness), aware that what seems calculated may be accidental—bordering on helpless. This would mean thinking differently about what we go on agonizing about, as "free will"; and reconsidering the starring role played by blame in our narratives of change. What alternatives to blaming and shaming might progressivism devise?

—

FRANK LOVES LIFTS—ELEVATORS—AND for a long time could watch for hours YouTube videos of them going up and down. We spent weekends at the train station, where the lift he called "green arrow" was usually free to ride as much as he liked; or, visiting a café whose "orange arrow," descending to a car park and rising to an art gallery, he played games with. He'd decide on a whim that only mummy, or only daddy, could come this time; or that one of us should go up and down by ourselves before returning. With these amused demands, Frank seemed to work through (as other children might enjoy games of hide-and-seek) his fear that one day we'd leave him and never return.

To isolate something *poetic* about Frank's ever-curious traversals, touchings, inquirings into, his variations on a theme, is to complicate overconvenient ideas of trauma. I'm thinking of a sentence I live by: Seamus Heaney's declaration that, for all its social and historical and political engagements, "poetry cannot afford to lose its fundamentally self-delighting inventiveness, its joy in being a process of language as well as a representation of things in the world."

Self-delighting inventiveness.

—

A LYRIC BY Louis MacNeice, "Mayfly," was described by a friend of mine, the poet and prose-writer Dai George, correctly I feel, as a "young man's poem"; it is, it turns out, a love poem about seizing the day. It stirs in me a dance of thoughts about my autistic son. It begins:

> Barometer of my moods today, mayfly,
> Up and down one among a million, one
> The same at best as the rest of the jigging mayflies,
> One only day of May alive beneath the sun.
>
> The yokels tilt their pewters and the foam
> Flowers in the sun beside the jeweled water.
> Daughter of the South, call the sunbeams home
> To nest between your breasts. The kingcups
> Ephemeral are gay gulps of laughter.
>
> Gulp of yellow merriment; cackle of ripples;
> Lips of the river that pout and whisper round
>     the reeds.
> The mayfly flirting and posturing over the water
> Goes up and down in the lift so many
>     times for fun.

—

WE REQUIRE ALTERNATIVES to the simplistic deficit-or-bonus model, by which neurodivergence is often economistically understood. I have learned a lot from the neurodiversity activist Nick Walker:

> Discourse and education on autism, in the academic and professional realms, has thus far been dominated by what I have termed the pathology paradigm. At the root of the pathology paradigm is the assumption that there is one "right" style of human neurocognitive functioning. Variations in neurocognitive functioning that diverge substantially from socially constructed standards of "normal"—including the variations that constitute autism—are framed within this paradigm as medical pathologies, as deficits, damage, or "disorders."
>
> In recent years a new paradigm has begun to emerge, which I refer to as the neurodiversity paradigm. The term neurodiversity, coined in the 1990s, refers to the diversity of human minds—the variations in neurocognitive functioning that manifest within the human species. Within the neurodiversity paradigm, neurodiversity is understood to be a form of human diversity that is subject to social dynamics—including the dynamics of oppression and systemic social power inequalities—similar to those dynamics that commonly occur around other forms of human diversity such as racial diversity or diversity of gender and sexual orientation.

The neurodiversity paradigm, as Walker puts it, sometimes redescribes what was once pathologized as a deficit as a superpower instead. It is as if we can only understand people different from us in terms of either inferiority or superiority. What was previously shamed and denigrated can be recuperated only as an enviable lagniappe—the parallel with race, envisioned as cultural capital, is clear. Yet talk of superpowers can hurt and not help neurodivergent people. Nancy

Doyle mentions "the inherent ableism and toxic positivity of expecting neurodivergent people to be superheroes," and an anonymous author speaks out in the pages of *Overland*:

> "Nothing about us without us" is a cherished maxim among disabled people—but what happens when the "us" is so diffuse that we're only ever representing a fraction of it? Although we may be united in a fight against ableism, what if our specific needs are so varied that our collective activism falls short?
>
> . . . In the past, the dominant narrative about autism was that of tragedy. Our disability has long been subjected to fear-mongering campaigns, bad-faith comparisons, eugenics, and all sorts of nasty rhetoric. Now, we're seeing a new narrative emerge that privileges autistic success stories. Its protagonists are quirkily divergent, possess impressive talents, are considered "useful" under capitalism, and reassure us that there's nothing to fear from autism.
>
> . . . I understand how this predicament has come about—again, through good intentions. To combat toxic negativity around autism, we've over-corrected with toxic positivity. This has been brewing for some time, regurgitated in how autism is deemed "a superpower" or "the next step of evolution" in ways that smoothly gloss over its challenges.
>
> When we speak about privilege relating to autism, this includes the usual factors such as race, gender, class or sexuality. But it also includes privileges specific to the disability—such as having low support needs, high cognitive and functional abilities, verbal speaking ability,

> good self-care and hygiene skills, and even being able to integrate into society and mask your autistic traits. After all, autism isn't an invisible disability for everyone: some of us are easily identified by things such as our atypical speech, social awkwardness and visible stimming, which affects our experience of the world. Those who display a higher degree of "normalcy"—even if it's conditional or comes at a high psychological toll—are often asked or selected to advocate on behalf of the whole community.

The point about who is *chosen*, either by those inside or outside a minoritized demographic, to advocate for that demographic, applies to race too. The actually or figuratively telegenic get the actual or figurative screen time. But this problem, of who gets to speak, is particularly acute for autistic people who may literally have no voice, or whose other disabilities restrict them to a private, not a public, life:

> Autistic people with intellectual disabilities make up a significant portion of our community, but they're rarely at the forefront of our collective activism.
>
> . . . Just as specific sub-groups deserve the option to forge their own safe spaces and self-determination—for autistic people of colour, autistic queer people, and so forth—we should take a similar view of autistic people with higher support needs, with severe and noticeable impairments, with a variety of co-occurring disabilities, who use augmentative and alternative communication (AAC), who've experienced 'intervention' therapies, who live in group homes, to name a few.

Perhaps controversially, I believe we should make space for the people who love us, too.

What does it mean for our ideas of identity, and ownership, that—asked, commissioned, to write a book about being Asian (which I am)—I find myself writing about my son, who is autistic while I am not? Could it be that our possessiveness around categories of minoritization is not only conceptually untenable (because those categories are porous, intersecting, and ever shifting) but also unattuned to *relational*, not self-focused, impulses, that we shouldn't apologize for but carefully, sensitively, embrace?

—

FRANK LEARNED A NEW PHRASE, "again and again," before his consonants—he had therapists helping him—firmed up. He began vigorously to inform us of his desire to ride Green Arrow not one or two or four times but "aden an aden." Like MacNeice's mayfly.

"Aden and aden"—*Eden*, it sounded like—was where Frank wanted to be; he specified it, as we engaged one of his enthusiasms (a better word, says Barry Prizant, than "obsessions," for an autistic child's foci)—as if securing the space of safety he required. When he runs in circles, or seeks pressure on the top of his head by standing on it, or nuzzling us, or headbutting a cushion; or when he rides the elevator, Frank is looking to *self-regulate*. An unpredictable world becomes bearable through an experience of sameness.

Repetition gets bad press. For Freud, the compulsion to

repeat—to both, for instance, suffer and seek out bad relationships, echoing how we've been badly parented—is really an impulse toward death. But repetition, and repetition-with-a-difference (of sounds, words, phrases), is also at the heart of poetry, and music, and perhaps all art.

Just like MacNeice's mayfly, Frank went "up and down in the lift so many times for *fun*." Discovering a new one at the library, he was magnetized, hurried over, serious-faced; then cried out with happiness, grinned, jumped up and down. It's this paradox that fascinates me. Where do we draw the line separating a coping mechanism from an experience of pure joy; can we really distinguish efforts at treading water from swimming out gaily, and fearlessly, to sea? It's patronizing to Frank, to consider his elevator adventures purely a form of mental insulation against reality. Or as fallow time that, were he neurotypical, he would experience more productively—whatever that means.

—

WHEN FRANK IS AROUND ELEVATORS, there's a mixture of joyousness, with absorbed scrutiny, that is enviable—I begin to understand why videos of autistic people enjoying their special interests are such a hit online. Many of us struggle with being desireless, distracted, unsure what we want. Once again—though in a different way from the "prickly white man" stereotype on TV—the autistic person stands for what we, as neurotypicals, desire. Box sets advertise themselves as "your next addiction": we wish to lose ourselves in an experience of total abandonment, or absorption—terminating that self-consciousness that keeps us wondering what to aim for and what the meaning of life really is. To watch an autistic person in the throes of—it seems like magic—a *reliable* fascination, is to imagine what it would be like to know exactly what we want, to know for good where happiness can be found; it is the vision, even, of a love affair that will never grow stale.

We're challenged by autistic enthusiasms, as by literature and perhaps especially poetry, to rethink ideas of productiveness, and the equations of time with money and work with life's meaning, which, over two hundred years after Max Weber's publication of *The Protestant Ethic and the Spirit of Capitalism*, continue to structure our lives.

How often do you feel you really should be *doing* something with your day, achieving something, constructing something to leave behind? You see something beautiful; it isn't enough to see and to share with those with you that evening in the mountains; you have to take a photograph of it, store the experience up like money in the bank. Or maybe you tweet about it too, again, to *do* something with the experience, to have it publicly validated. What's the alternative? Memories degrade. Yet this desperation, to hold on to the passing moment, may be precisely what pushes it out of reach.

Romantic poets idealized birds, and birdsong. Birds seemed to sing for pure joy, no other reason (this isn't true, they sing to mate, mark out territory, to express aggression, but humans needed to ignore this, to create an ideal, during times when industrialization was hugely transforming society). Birds also, unlike poets writing poems about them, are content to sing without recording their songs, without being praised, memorialized, and defined by them.

What would a birdwatcher be like, who didn't make a list of the birds they'd seen? Who existed purely within their encounter with those beautiful creatures, without introducing an act of administration, of box-ticking, to validate their hobby?

—

THERE IS SOMETHING SCANDALOUS, then, about Frank and the mayfly going up and down in the lift for fun. They should be doing something else with their lives. They should be growing, learning, evolving, accommodating themselves to reality, challenging themselves . . . To parent an autistic child one must resist a discourse of original sin, that ableist voice (I'm thinking of a letter from a doctor, recommending twenty-five hours of ABA—Applied Behavior Analysis—therapy a week, to prevent Frank from *regressing*) that says your child's most basic, deepest impulses are *wrong*, and to be countermanded.

This is a story even neurotypicals tell themselves—or have been told by others, fervently. South Asians are said to pressure their children to excel academically, toward the goal of becoming (ideally) a doctor. I see Frank going up and down in the lift, and hear my parents insisting that he can't be autistic, that there is nothing "wrong" with him, he is a genius, that he will overcome, that, in my father's words, *he will change the way people live*; and within me a wave of protectiveness curdles into oppositional rage.

I don't know if I'm talking about Frank, or myself, or the version of me, Vid 2.0, my parents see him as, when I shout (in my mind): *He doesn't have to do any of these things. Just let him be.*

—

DESCRIBING KINGCUPS AS "ephemeral," MacNeice toys with the Greek taxonomic name for the mayfly, *ephemeroptera*. It means short-lived, or more specifically, that which lives only a day. To understand how radically joyous the act of this literary mayfly is, rising and falling over the water, we need to recognize that the day it spends this way isn't the equivalent of a weekend. It is its entire existence. Or as MacNeice says, "one only day of May alive beneath the sun." If there's a fleet of poems in which a male poet advises the woman he loves to seize the day (which means, to have sex with him), MacNeice deepens things by alluding to the mayfly's history as an icon for the brevity of life. Aristotle: "This creature is exceptional not only in regard to the duration of its existence, whence it receives its name"; the English poet George Crabbe compared newspapers to mayflies, because so much news is just foam and froth: "Such are these base ephemeras, so born / To die before the next revolving morn."

---

THE MAYFLY FASCINATES US, then, not for what it is, but for what it tells us of our own mortality. I want to compare this with neurotypical misunderstandings of autistic people. On the one hand, we have the figure I mentioned, a white man whose behaviors, and the free ride he gets for them, expose our culture. On the other, there is the long-standing misrepresentation of the autistic person as someone with no sense of other people's independent existence. (A writer I admire, Adam Phillips, cites the discredited work of Frances Tustin, to this end.) This image of isolation is clearly necessary to our imaginations, just as the image of the mayfly or the singing bird is necessary. It tells us of our deepest fears; perhaps, even, about the atomizing effect of late-stage capitalism, and how we're isolated from each other by our private concerns, to the point of feeling that we can't communicate.

But this is the neurotypical mind talking about itself. It has nothing to do with autistic people. It has nothing to do with Roddy, or Frank, or indeed those with higher support needs: those who may be nonverbal, or speak with the aid of special devices, or require lifelong care, but who still have rich inner lives they *can* express (under no obligation) to the rest of us, if only we choose to listen.

—

IT IS, IN SHORT, a form of appropriation: yet this book, in which I look at poems and bounce back from them into my own life and that of my family, is necessarily engaged in, I hope, more defensible kinds of appropriation. Our conversations on this topic are confused. The appropriation of minoritized creativeness for monetary gain—notably, white people co-opting Black styles—obscures other microexperiences of appropriation inevitable to the sort of relational beings that we are.

To be angry—to experience that dopamine rush—on someone's else behalf, online or offline, may also turn into appropriation; the shifting, of our most feted literary genre, from fiction (in which it is now felt that the author steps irresponsibly out of their own lane, into the experiences of others) to nonfiction, autofiction, memoir, in no way removes the problem of appropriation, because the writer is still, like a social media influencer using footage of others in a viral video, annexing others to their own story—perhaps in a more direct and violent way. When I read a poem, I may do so appropriatively at one moment, before passing, within the complex encounter with otherness that reading comprises, to another, unforeseen, level of contact. Simplistic ideas of ownership cannot keep pace with the unavoidably relational, interdependent, momentum of thought, nor the transnational circulation of ideas.

Let's also consider experiences that one *is* supposed to unproblematically inhabit; to inherit, as both trauma and cultural capital—as if I had a PhD not only in poetry but also in being a Sri Lankan Tamil. Some say this is what I should write about—what they *want* to hear about; many publishers liked the idea of a racialized memoir, only to balk at poetry. "As a Sri Lankan Tamil . . . ": I don't want to write this sentence anymore. It claims an impossible expertise: not the humane half knowledge that begins or amends a conversation, but something more absolute, wanting the last word. Are we ever really experts on ourselves?

Psychology suggests otherwise. "Lived experience" is more nebulous, tougher to grasp or interpret, than we wish to admit—perhaps *especially* for those minoritized groups (Sri Lankan Tamils, yes, and also autistic people) that understandably want to claim, now, the right to tell their own stories.

—

MACNEICE'S APPROPRIATION, or idealization, of the mayfly feels harmless: he recognizes what he's doing, with the ingenious, and overt, metaphor, "barometer of my moods."

The insect becomes an engram of his own emotional ups and (corresponding to the "lift" image) downs. When happy, we proclaim ourselves in ways—this is what MacNeice's poem is doing—that we *know* will seem unreasonable when our mood changes. Those of us with chronic mental health issues may feel as if we are several different people. "The world of the happy man," said Ludwig Wittgenstein—I repeat myself; I repeat him—"is a different one from that of the unhappy man." Except for some, there is a happy person inside, and an unhappy one, and they keep changing places.

—

IS THIS WHY a second voice enters MacNeice's poem, creating a dialogue? The poet begins by speaking to the mayfly, and will end by directly addressing his lover, whose first appearance in the poem was as the "Daughter of the South." For the moment, the mayfly itself speaks, on behalf of the young and carefree:

> 'When we are grown up we are sure to alter
> Much for the better, to adopt solider creeds;
> The kingcup will cease proffering his cup
> And the foam will have blown from the beer and
>     the heat no longer dance
> And the lift lose fascination and the May
> Change her tune to June—but the trouble with
>     us mayflies
> Is that we never have the chance to be grown up.'

They never have the chance, but what of
  time they have
They stretch out taut and thin and ringing clear;
So we, whose strand of life is not much more,
Let us too make our time elastic and
Inconsequently dance above the dazzling wave.

This book was published in 1935, just four years before World War II, an event MacNeice would analyze as both a poet and a journalist. So when he writes "solider creeds," my eyelid flickers and I misread, "soldier," seeing afresh those mayflies dying in their millions. How many young men never had the chance to "grow up"? British recruits were meant to be at least eighteen years old, but in reality, thousands of boys as young as fourteen raced off to war. This is a poem by someone haunted by mass death, and wary of another global conflict looming. Its attitude resembles that of the flappers of the 1920s—their carefree abandonment to pleasure premised on the need to block out, erase, numb oneself to, the knowledge of millions killed and yet to be killed.

—

GIVEN THE SUBJECT of this book—South Asian identity, or the empty space it should inhabit—I want to discuss something hard to talk about: the resistance of my Sri Lankan Tamil family to Frank's diagnosis. What began as outright rejection continues to smolder as a milder, often invoked, resistance to diagnostic categories.

I speak of comparison—the defining mode of this book—and its bad double: appropriation. My parents, as you'll remember from the introduction, repeatedly compare Frank to me, applying the narrative of heroic intellectual progress which emerges from the suffering of Sri Lankan Tamils and the imaginative constructs they devised, to conceptualize, and in some cases genuinely stimulate, a means of social mobility both within Sri Lanka and outside it. Our local preschool offers Frank four free half days a week—having diagnosed a "developmental delay." My parents see autism as a stigma. Being Sri Lankan Tamil, they've always feared that in some way they, I, Frank, will be found out and marked out, have everything taken away from us. Historic traumas persist as terrors become contagious; as obsessive thoughts in the individual mind; even, as conversations that repeat almost word for word, as if we were actors in a play.

When Jenny and I worry that Frank, being neurodivergent, will have to mask, adapt, memorize learned scripts and desirable behaviors, in order to thrive, a voice seems to return out of the past; that voice reminding me that England wasn't filled with people who looked like me or acted like me, that I must alter my accent and personality and work twice as hard as others, not even to succeed, but to be conditionally accepted.

In this way, Frank—the autistic person—is once again disallowed his own space. He has been co-opted into not a cultural but a subcultural, a familial, psychodrama.

—

MACNEICE'S POEM ENDS by saying we shouldn't

> put too much on the sympathy of things,
> The dregs of drink, the dried cups of flowers,
> The pathetic fallacy of the passing hours
> When it is we who pass them—hours of stone,
> Long rows of granite sphinxes looking on.
>
> It is we who pass them, we the circus masters
> Who make the mayflies dance, the lapwings lift
> their crests;
> The show will soon shut down, its gay-rags gone,
> But when this summer is over let us die together,
> I want always to be near your breasts.

Neurodivergent people with "low-affect" expressions—matching the popular misreading of East Asian faces—are sometimes stereotyped as unfeeling and empty, or reservoirs of inscrutable mystery: "granite sphinxes looking on."

The pathetic fallacy, as theorized by the Victorian art-critic and cultural sage John Ruskin, concerns writing that misrepresents nature by saturating it with our emotions; although he defends this literary procedure as a *representation of* the viral, overweening, uncontrollable spread of feeling, leaping out of our minds to reshape all a tortured person sees. When a poet describes a sea of "cruel, crawling foam,"

> the foam is not cruel, neither does it crawl. The state of mind which attributes to it these characters of a living creature is one in which the reason is unhinged by grief.

And when the Romantic poet Samuel Taylor Coleridge describes the last red leaf tumbling from a tree as *dancing*, he "has a morbid, that is to say, a so far false, idea about the leaf: he fancies a life in it, and will, which there are not; confuses its powerlessness with choice, its fading death with merriment, and the wind that shakes it with music."

To think hard about Frank and the lift is to reconsider the relationship between matter and spirit, mechanism and joy. To Frank, lifeless objects—elevators, buttons, lights, twigs moved by the wind across his path, so he either shrieks with fear or giggles—have often seemed like "living creatures." Returning to Roddy's poem, and what he does with the normally lifeless, objectifying pronoun "it," I realize that for him, as for Frank, the border between life and death isn't clear. And this is no delusion, for even a human being is but a collection of particles in an ever-changing pattern. We are, as the Zen writer, lecturer, and—he preferred the term—entertainer Alan Watts liked to put it, not separate beings but one aspect, spark, ripple, of a universe that has come to the point of scrutinizing itself. Watts draws on the Hindu idea of divine play—the whole universe is Brahman, playing hide-and-seek.

MacNeice knows the feelings he ascribes to mayflies and lapwings originate in his mind. As this imagined world drops away, the poem reveals itself as a love-lyric, addressing the woman whose "breasts" he wishes to be near. Which suggests maternal, not romantic, love: the desire of a child to be embraced and nourished by their parent. Is this why I see Frank in this poem? It isn't just the lifts. It is the transformation in me that parenting Frank has brought about: the recognition, through him, of the childlike intensities of feeling that shape all our lives, which we struggle to regulate, let alone understand, though we don't all face the problem as perpetually, as heroically, from day to day and minute to minute, as an autistic person does.

—

THERE ARE THINGS we try to forget, but which persist; and things, events, people, we'd like to be more interested in, to escape toward, out of a tortured past, except memories keep dragging us back, and down.

"And the lift lose fascination." The Latin, *fascinus*, refers to—according to the *OED*—"a charm, enchantment, spell, witchcraft." I spoke of our desire to be spellbound, to be wholly absorbed. But this also frightens us. The person entirely given over to one experience seems to have discarded all others. More than that, they appear to have no use for other people—for you and for me. In finding exactly what they need, their own personal *summum bonum*, the wellspring of all pleasure, they have become either godlike or monstrous. They have seceded from the human collective.

What's remarkable about MacNeice's poem is its redemption of repetition, its redefinition of the "rigid" and "inflexible"—words Frank's occupational therapists applied, to my chagrin, to his play—as a means of making time "elastic." I see within Frank's elevator games, his engrossed attention to numbers, letters, and colors, a repertoire of brilliant and evolving variations on a theme. As he plays with his doll's house containing a lift; or the lift he and his granddad made together out of Lego, and which can be rebuilt different ways; or swoops down the slide after pressing an imaginary button first, as if dropping from one floor to the next, the smile on his face rhymes with—is repeated by, though with a difference—the smile on mine.

# *Impediment*

Silence, and repetition. For a long time Frank didn't talk. He opened and closed doors and didn't respond to us. Gradually he accrued a team of specialists to help with his motor skills, imaginative play, above all with speech. As he struggled to reproduce consonants and vowels—bursting, sometimes, into tears—I, blocking out his pain, thought of my own childhood.

If I am a writer, not a talker—a reader maybe, not a listener—it is through growing up with a speech impediment. My parents, told by their GP that I was deaf in one ear and developmentally delayed (shown a cartoon horse in a field, I shouted "cow!"), were skeptical. For them it was a "lisp" such as my uncle had growing up, and a cousin too. Back in Sri Lanka, they said, these things weren't problems—children grew out of them.

But the impediment remained. At nursery school I couldn't pronounce *r* sounds. "Yainbow," I'd say, instead of "rainbow." The ability of some to roll their *r*'s still feels supernatural. My parents sent me to speech classes: an uninnocent decision (that is also difficult to say, I seem to gravitate toward such dissonances, as if revisiting a trauma to master it). My sister was already trained in elocution. Eradicating from their children's voices any hint of a South Asian accent (this is why, they claimed, they never taught us Tamil), my parents were trying to protect us. Which made those lessons, those hours spent laboriously coordinating toward communicativeness my resisting mouth- and tongue-muscles, a version of the double erasure experienced by Marc Shell in mid-twentieth-century Canada:

> For Grace McCullough and Agnes Birmingham, whose 1925 textbook provided my school with its guiding principles, "correcting speech defects and foreign accent" amounted to the same thing.
>
> So I was taught in Lower Westmount that I had *two* sorts of speech impediments and that they were interrelated. The first impediment was *general* disfluency in speaking *all* languages, a problem from which stutterers suffered—or so said the experts. The second impediment was my particular inability to speak a *particular* language with the proper accent.

If minoritized communities, lower classes and immigrants, train themselves in received pronunciation, it's through knowing what it's like to be persecuted and prosecuted for the tiniest divergence from the norm; language itself, one's means of expression, pullulates with prejudice. Tamil, which my parents didn't teach me, has morphed into an absent presence, a revenant pressure, on the Queen's English—a brimming acrolect—which I was taught and have sought to diversify. How flabbergasted strangers still are, that a brown person speaks as I do! But there's also that moment of doubt, in the sliding gaze of those who *do* know me, when my tutored enunciation begins to glitch. When the consonants go back to malfunctioning. Elsewhere and elsewhen, intonations from a language I was never taught begin to intrude, warping English sentence-sounds into shapes inherited from my parents despite their linguistic cordon sanitaire.

No process of deracination is total. In so many tiny and not so tiny ways, the past returns; if a language is lost a contour of emphasis remains, sneaking like a virus into the DNA of the sentences I've carried across the world, from Sri Lanka to the UK to the US. Whenever I go back to my parents to check the pronunciation of words or names in my writing, or when my father and I translate poems into English, my mother says with regret: "We should have taught you Tamil." The decision not to teach me some things, and the helpless involuntary transference of much else—beliefs, prejudices, talk-styles, think-styles, migrating from parent to child—is as dizzying to consider as empire: the immeasurable history without which I (and possibly you too) wouldn't exist.

In the Bible, the Ephraimites, who can't pronounce the word "shibboleth"—"sibboleth," they cry, with, I imagine, the compensatory fortissimo, the egregious vehemence, with which I yelled "yainbow!"—are killed for it. Seamus Heaney alludes to this in "Broagh":

> its low tattoo
> among the windy boortrees
> and rhubarb-blades

ended almost
suddenly, like that last
*gh* the strangers found
difficult to manage.

That would be a "tattoo" in the sense of, a drumbeat. But the sense of an indelible mark on the flesh, a stigma impossible to efface, is there too. In this case, pronouncing "Broagh" properly means you belong somewhere (in Ulster) the powers that be (those British strangers) can't dominate. They'll find the natives "hard to manage."

—

SPEECH BEING UNMANAGEABLE, I turned to the written page, and was teased at school, like many others, for "reading the dictionary." I persuaded my father to buy the micrographic edition of the complete *OED* (it was £160 or so), though he feared the minuscule print would ruin my eyes. It came with a magnifying glass satisfyingly shaped like a gun—with a honey-yellow trigger for switching on and off a useless, tiny bulb.

Even now, if I close my eyes and concentrate, I can remember the smell of my mother's chicken-and-potato curry wafting up the stairs, and the television in the sitting room dully booming through the floorboards, and the feel of half-kneeling on my mattress with the dictionary open beside me, heavy as a person—a lover.

—

THOUGH HE STRUGGLED with other sounds, substituting *d* for consonants he couldn't manage, Frank never suffered, as I did and still do, from *rhotacism*. Red! he shouts—or *Is that right?!*—having already achieved something beyond me. His phoneme is sharper and clearer than mine and always will be. No amount of introspection can remedy the deficit shared by my lips and tongue and mouth-muscles, it is irreparable: a micro-incompetence resurrected whenever I open my mouth to speak. Wrestling with *r* sounds as a child, I came to a primordial distrust in the world, matching my physical clumsiness—the feeling objects wouldn't behave in my hands but would spill, break, ooze into nooks and crannies and hide there; but also the feeling that my parents, ignorant of England's rules, couldn't shield me from embarrassment. All of this was compressed and compacted into my failure to make myself understood.

I've published a poem about this called "As a child," containing the word "mirror," a special horror to me (like "horror" itself). That double *r* is quicksand. Out of it I can't get free. My mother, leaving me to my first speech lesson, found me sat before a mirror, crying inconsolably as I struggled to pronounce *r* sounds over and over again—scrutinized by my teacher, but also asked to self-surveil, watching my reflection for errors. When Frank was recommended for ABA therapy, which many autistic people consider abusive—though the families of those with severer needs may disagree, and they also deserve a hearing—I read about children being pressured to make eye contact or not to stim, and remembered the abjection of my own speech lessons.

Vladimir Nabokov, that wonderful prose stylist, couldn't

speak English as he could Russian. So his interviews featured typed questions and typed responses. He too replaced speech with writing. This means that when you read one of his magisterially alliterative sentences, you're encountering stammers marvelously transposed: a defect refashioning itself as virtuosity. As Shell remarks,

> what *sometimes* develops from the mental effort needed to deal with stuttering by way of both intra- and interlinguistic synonymy and personal substitution has certain rewards. After all, "compensating" for the difficulties of dis-ease, if not of dis-ability, is often a precondition for, if not a trigger of, genius. Victor Shklovsky, the Russian Formalist literary critic, claimed that intellectual hurdles can be as good for the mind as physical ones are for the body. Was it Shakespeare's near-inability to *stop* punning that helped make him the writer he was? William Butler Yeats used to say that it was his dyslexia that made *him* the singsong poet he became.

If my speech impediment has guided my feeling for poetry, it has also promoted the idea that our creativity comes of our pain and somehow redeems it. I've a hunger to pursue this in the most pigheaded and no doubt reductive way. So, as Keats wrote of Milton that his disability shaped his imagination ("it can scarcely be conceived how Milton's blindness might here aid the magnitude of his conceptions as a bat in a large gothic vault"), I like to consider Alexander Pope's physical disadvantages outfaced by the crystalline rigor of his couplets; and, returning to speech impediments, the Northern Irish poet Ciaran Carson seems to me another stylist whose experiments issue from a self-consciousness to do with speech.

Carson had a bad stutter that disappeared when he played the flute or sang. Growing up with a speech impediment, one avoids words that function as obstacles, replacing them with others. This means you're already a writer, an editor, standing at a remove from your sentences and considering how they might be tweaked. It isn't possible to open your mouth before engaging your brain. An obstacle can be redefined. Carson's stylistic breakthrough, 1987's *The Irish for No*, came up with a garrulous, pretend-slovenly, contrapurposive long line, which could include, no doubt, sundry atrocity-details, and digress essayistically, but also suggests the stutterer's dream, of overtaking one's hindrance once and for all and riding a torrent of talk whose foaming energy, once begun, is invulnerable to cessation. Absorbed into an ampler sensorium, individual sounds become enabling, not disabling:

*I wandered homesick-lonely through that Saturday of*
*silent Tallinn*
*When a carillon impinged a thousand raining quavers on*
*my ear, tumbling*

*Dimly from immeasurable heights into imaginary brazen*
*gong-space, trembling*
*Dimpled in their puddled, rain-drop halo-pools,*
*concentrically assembling.*

"Eesti," from *Opera Et Cetera* (1996)

In Carson's poems, internalized political terrors (and real-world checkpoints) are envisioned as a return of the repressed: "I was trying to complete a sentence in my head, but it kept stuttering. // . . . Why can't I escape? Every move is punctuated." The long line breaks into short sentences—the gasping units of meaning, of the stutterer; elsewhere, Carson goes the other way, writing very short lines that fetishize the experience of apocopation, entrapment within one's own voice, and do with it something gruelingly innovative. In *Dubliners*, James Joyce writes of hearing "the rain impinge upon the earth." Alluding to and improvising on this phrase, Carson describes the sound of bells as "raindrop halo-pools," a carillon which "impinged a thousand raining quavers on my ear."

This is the hypersensitized sonic universe of the stutterer, where speech risks fraying into disconnected sounds. These phonemes "impinge" violently even as the speaker (the Sri Lankan Canadian poet Rienzi Crusz writes, instead, of "insurgent rain") undertakes a force which, on the brink of forming words, becomes perversely babelic and askance (as if it were possible to stub one's tongue instead of one's toe).

—

PROBLEMS ARISE—AS I MENTIONED, regarding neurodivergence—when we reclassify what once were considered deficits as sources of strength; I'm reminded of immigrants, and specifically Sri Lankan Tamils, ferociously metabolizing all obstacles, converting every problem into its own solution. A mountain of lemons is turned into a thriving lemonade business. I would prefer to break with the disability-genius paradigm entirely, but family tiffs about Frank reveal how difficult this can be.

When I read the dictionary, was it only and always as a cure for my ineptitudes of speech? Must we read our strongest drives in terms of insecurity and power, or is there such a thing as pure curiosity, a mind unfolding like a flower?

I didn't read to look up what I didn't understand, but to pursue words completely new to me. I wouldn't say the concepts or experiences behind those words, since the sound-shape is what mattered. Above and beyond the borrowed, skewwhiff, and in its own way marvelous, English my immigrant parents deployed, the *OED* provided fascinating letter-combinations wholly and wholesomely new to me, whose pronunciation I might also have learned but preferred to imagine for myself. A particular acoustic impression was linked with the printed signifier and could not be dislodged. "Albeit," I thought, was *all-bate*, and a know-it-all at school corrected, without a trace of irony, my mishearing of "pedantic"—I assumed a long *pee* sound at the start. An English teacher said I hunted out new words as a pig does truffles.

Some came not from the *OED* but a Reader's Digest "reverse dictionary" resembling a thesaurus but really an aspirational tome for replacing a normal word with something more thrillingly and impressively esoteric. I remember as clearly as the pain of sticking my thumb inquisitively in our Peugeot's cigarette lighter my discovery in that pompous red book of "recherché," a word incredible to behold and attempt with fumbling tongue and lips. Which I didn't think of as French: my fascination was with the *English* language, its capaciousness and acceptance of the foreign; an arena in which I could be confident of my originality, if nothing else. W. H. Auden says that, stranded on a desert island, he would choose for his reading "a good dictionary rather than the greatest literary masterpiece imaginable, for, in relation to its readers, a dictionary is absolutely passive and may legitimately be read in an infinite number of ways." What dictionaries have provided for me is the word-lover's experience of omnicompetence, of endless, because merely potential and unrealized, power. In that book of secret lore, words were possible incantations, and their meanings, graftable into stories and essays (and eventually poems), held out the promise of understanding, to a child whose immigrant parents never seemed sure how to act in a still unfamiliar country, about which they struggled to answer their son's endless and no doubt infuriating questions.

—

MY SHOCKED MOTHER never took me back to that elocution teacher who made me cry. I studied under Mrs. J instead, who was soft-spoken and kindly, though in the habit of comparing me unfavorably with my sister, who once reduced an audience to tears with her performance of Wilde's *Salomé*:

> Jokanaan, thou wert the man that I loved alone among men. All other men were hateful to me. But thou wert beautiful! Thy body was a column of ivory set upon feet of silver. It was a garden full of doves and lilies of silver. It was a tower of silver decked with shields of ivory. There was nothing in the world so white as thy body.

*There was nothing in the world so white as thy body*. I wasn't made for such performances; as well as the impediment, there was, said Mrs. J, my mild asthma, making me breathless—enforcing an inappropriate caesura—partway through a sentence or a verse-line. She marked with a little penciled *p* the moments to pause either for breath or for emphasis. Years later, during my first Oxford tutorial, another Northern Irish poet, Tom Paulin, tried to convince us (a group of skeptical eighteen- and nineteen-year-olds) that the poetry of Christina Rossetti contained invisible pauses—moments, he said, of feminist strength: "An opal holds a fiery spark; / but a *flint* holds fire."

My emphasis; but, really, the italics aren't mine: Rossetti shapes the voice-contour to linger on "flint." Gerard Manley Hopkins, who admired her, pasted stress marks into poems. The reader was to read them aloud, perform them, according to his musical score. I love Hopkins, but this is controlling. Rossetti's form of persuasion, her encoding of a voice within the lines, is subtler. I knew what Tom was talking about, seeing in my mind that penciled *p*, just where he, and before him Mrs. J, said it would be. That was the day I became a literary critic.

—

I FIND IT IMPOSSIBLE to separate my literary interests—reading, teaching, writing poetry or writing criticism—from my upbringing. However apparently abstract my essays, or however deracinated my poems may seem to be, there's an underlying predicament that, since it outgoes the usual immigrant narratives and South Asian clichés, continues to resist articulation. (For it to be articulated, I need to find the right words, but there also has to exist an audience ready to understand.) At what point does a parent's emphasis on academic accomplishment magically morph, away from vicarious careerism, into a passion—an unworldly vocation—that will shape their child's life?

Or, are my talents with words a form of revenge, on England and on English, for humiliating both me (when I tried, as a child, to speak it) and my parents in so many unforgettable ways? Cathy Park Hong writes of her Korean mother's English as a "crush of piano keys":

> As my mother spoke, I watched the white person, oftentimes a woman, put on a fright mask of strained tolerance: wide eyes frozen in trapped patience, smile widened in condescension. As she began responding to my mother in a voice reserved for toddlers, I stepped in.
>
> From a young age, I learned to speak for my mother as authoritatively as I could. Not only did I want to dispel the derision I saw behind that woman's eyes, I wanted to shame her with my sobering fluency for thinking what she was thinking. I have been partly drawn to writing, I realize, to judge those who have unfairly judged my family; to prove that I've been watching this whole time.

How indelible the memories are, of my mother struggling laboriously to make herself understood; my father, even—who'd prissily correct her English—taking me to buy our first computer, flummoxed by the salesman's unctuous patter and the small green boxes, the insufficient space, where he was supposed to write in ballpoint the letters of his extravagantly long Tamil name. He marched out of the shop: no one was going to make a fool of him! Only to return with his tail between his legs, because, without a computer, how would I get ahead at school—I knew this was on my parents' minds, I overheard them. And so my father made nice. The countless tiny defeats my parents experienced every day, because the language wasn't theirs: Did I feel that by mastering English, I could stick up for them? Or was it the fear of being treated as they were treated—would I do anything to avoid that?

—

AS A TEENAGER doing my GCSEs, I bunked off school and would lie on my bed facing the wall, refusing to speak. My parents didn't know why. I'd faced racism at school, and not only from other students: a teacher told a boy not to sit next to me, in case the mud I'd clearly fallen in, flat on my face, stained his uniform. But I don't think this was the reason. I suspect it was a test regarding the powers of speech and silence; also, a testing of the conditionality (I feared) of my parents' love. That I excelled was so often uppermost in their minds. My brilliance was supposed to continue the Tamil mission—onward and upward. If I dropped the ball, or refused to play, would I still be special to them?

My parents passed this test, and others. (Tamils don't fail tests.) In Sri Lanka, they faced the opposite of affirmative action: as a minority unfairly (it was thought) well represented in higher education and white-collar employment, their children had to score more highly in examinations than others to succeed. When I told my parents that I hated my speech lessons and wanted to stop, they said, "But what about your akka form for university? You have to put *something* on it!"

*Akka* in Tamil means "sister"—my sister was "Vani-akka," and a pillow-cover I half inched from her and clung to became "Akka pillow" (white, soft, with gray, chewed corners). So, never questioning what this "akka form" was, I associated it blurrily with my brilliant sister who was now at Oxford studying human sciences. Only when applying to university myself, years later—filling out my UCAS (Universities and Colleges Admissions Service) form—did the lightbulb switch on over my head. Until 1993, UCAS was the UCCA. That's what my mother was trying to say all along. My UCCA form.

—

MY MOTHER'S MALAPROPISMS are a running joke in our family. "Strawberry mouse," she says, instead of "mousse"; "I am a spring bird," instead of "chicken." Speaking with a thick, to some incomprehensible, accent, she was bullied at work: her boss mocked the "wuh-wuh" noise she uses as a space-filler between English words, and, refusing to promote her, suggested that in meetings no one would understand what she was trying to say. During the grievance process my mother was asked if the bullying was racist. It was a point of pride with her to say no.

I'm nervous of telephones. Whenever my mother took a call, I had to leave the room; as her voice strove upriver, and she laboriously spelled out words letter by letter—"*R* is for Robert. *A* is for Arthur. *V* is for Victoria"—I identified not with her but with the bemused white person on the other end. I used to wince at restaurants when she asked for her food a "little spicy," meaning, *much* spicier, and the waiter thought she meant "not very." She's always trying to make everything easy and everyone happy, but it's exactly this hypertinkering that causes problems.

And yet, if you asked me about her accent, I'd tell you I can't hear it. I squint acoustically, trying to focus, but it's no good. For hers is the voice in my blood, running along my dreams—it is for me what the burbling of the Derwent was for Wordsworth. I've a recurrent nightmare where she, as in my teens, nags me to cease hiding in my bedroom with my face turned to the wall and to return to school. With each year that passes, my objections grow more absurd. "But I'm in my twenties, I'm a DPhil student, I don't have to go to school!" "But I teach at Harvard, I'm thirty-nine, I've already completed all my exams!" But she just keeps talking and talking, in that unstoppered, unstoppable, voice. "You're not listening," I cry, but there she is, as always, butting in. "Can I just say." "I am sorry to say this, but . . . " "You must go to school and be twice as good as the white children, if you want to be given the same as them."

—

THE PERSONAL STATEMENT on my UCAS form didn't mention my limited accomplishments in speech and drama. Instead, it was filled with high-minded talk of "Art," with a capital *A*. This was because my recovery from silence and my eventual return to school and exams, was made possible by Oscar Wilde, and his aestheticism was in my bloodstream—a desperate infusion.

*There was nothing in the world so white as thy body.*

I could not recite those lines as my sister could, but could in other ways emulate Wilde, taking this to absurd extremes. In an essay, I wrote that, reading a book, "we are but violins on which the work of Art must play." (I know nothing about classical music and cannot play the violin.) Wilde wore a green carnation in his buttonhole; buying yellow ones from the supermarket, I altered their color with a felt-tip pen.

I'd read somewhere, perhaps in Richard Ellmann's biography, that Wilde could speak off the cuff in poetic meter: hexameters, blank verse. This seemed like magic to me, an armor of elegance no humiliation could pierce. I didn't make the connection with my impediment, speech lessons, or the fact that Wilde, once an ungainly Irish child nicknamed the "grey crow" (with, it was said, dirty skin) learned to flourish in the teeth of his enemies by becoming more English than the English. Nor did I recognize the conditions under which I'd first discovered his novel, *The Picture of Dorian Gray*: that force of Tamil aspiration causing my father to stock our house with literary classics neither he nor my mother had read. Of all the characters, I wanted to be Wilde's stand-in, Lord Henry Wotton, even when *he* says he'd rather be Dorian himself:

> I wish I could change places with you, Dorian. The world has cried out against us both, but it has always worshipped you. It always will worship you. You are the type of what the age is searching for, and what it is afraid it has found. I am so glad that you have never done anything, never carved a statue, or painted a picture, or produced

> anything outside of yourself! Life has been your art. You have set yourself to music. Your days are your sonnets.

What fascinates me is how the opposition between art and life also takes us to praise, encouragement, safety, and the idea that our paramount experiences are beyond our control. Live learnedly, exquisitely, so when your mind wanders, it won't be into fantasies of harm, or a litany of excruciatingly recalled defeats, but a world of sumptuous perceptions. Wotton urges Dorian on, just as my parents did to me and continue to, insisting I'm special and unique. Such is the pressure they now place on Frank.

—

I BEGAN USING dictionaries the way you're meant to when I started reading difficult poetry, and writing words I didn't understand in the front of books to look them up later. Turning to Paul Muldoon's *Poems 1968–1998*, I find the following words (only five; I must have given up quickly) scribbled in the front:

*sward* *trew*
*dulse*
*jennet* *perruque*

There are words we look up and remember because they approach our interests, and words a poet commits to memory (or a notebook) since they shine and vibrate as something usable. These can be quite ordinary, unspectacular signifiers—or those above or below or on the adjacent page to the one you went hunting for. You begin to flip through the dictionary; everywhere, nouns and adjectives and verbs leap out with an inexhaustible suggestiveness. This is what it meant to me to read that fabulous book: an appetitive delight, combining amazement at what was strange and different to me with a happily growing sense of my own capabilities.

—

TWO WORDS IN PARTICULAR still flummox me: I hate how they conjoin with a half, a sloppy, rhyme, one of them double-activating the dreaded *r* sound. But they aren't words that appear in the dictionary.

What a nexus of anxieties, compensations, spring forth when a South Asian must share their own obscure, polysyllabic name!

Sometimes I feel like a large soft brown Pokémon waddling from place to place, squawking its nomenclature. *Vidyan Ravinthiran* is chewy, sing-songy. The rhyme emerges as a failed, halfway assertiveness: I begin to materialize as a person of consequence (my names support each other sonically, they announce me), then break off, apologizing either implicitly or explicitly for these weird, wrongfooting words. Asked my name, I prevaricate for two reasons: on the one hand, I think whoever's listening won't get it right; there's also the feeling I'll fudge it myself, given those *r*'s (the fatal flaw is within my own name, it is *inside me*). Also, since only at my sister's wedding did I learn—from a cheat sheet for guests—that "Vidyan" is supposed to be pronounced "Vi-thee-un." A change I haven't made, for it would mean reckoning with the fact that until the age of sixteen it wasn't only everyone else, but me too, getting my name wrong.

—

THOSE SCRAWLED LISTS in the front of old books suggest an aesthetic of control; a belief in poems as word-constructions, not self-expression, and a yearning for life itself to become something, as it was for Wilde, exquisitely contrived. My background, the self-consciousness of my tutored enunciation, is relevant; and at the heart of it all, the formative experience of the dictionary, of looking up, looking things up, as a sort of transcendence. I intend the wordplay. For looking down at the thin, turned pages through that insufficient magnifying glass was like the habit, common across cultures, of raising, at the crucial moment, your eyes to the sky; an instinctive consultation of an external power. The dictionary was mine, it was for me, it was in my corner, and its creative prompt was both unforeseeable in nature and eerily guaranteed, whenever I, with difficulty, picked it up. It, not me, was where writing came from and what writing was made of; yet this wasn't alienation, but intimacy.

Although I no longer build poems around individually fascinating words, it's always a happy occurrence to check meanings in the dictionary, and find the line you've written is deeper than you thought and alive with crosscurrents you had not predicted. A definition is to the poet a usable instance, a moment of power, a guarantor of the process of sense-making the creative artist is, like the lexicographer, committed to—however mischievously or vagariously. Yet the dictionary also reveals language as an endlessly fecund medium, and that's reassuring. It is like the child playing with his mother's body and rediscovering its lovely elastic presence, the springily responsive give and take that might go on forever.

I'm thinking here not only of the believer looking up to the sky but also the child looking up from the breast to its mother's eyes for that reassurance which is also, Wordsworth tells us in *The Prelude*, the realization of a spiritual bond. Blessed is the infant,

> Nursed in his Mother's arms, who sinks to sleep
> Rocked on his Mother's breast; who with his soul
> Drinks in the feelings of his Mother's eye!
> For him, in one dear Presence, there exists
> A virtue which irradiates and exalts
> Objects through widest intercourse of sense.
> No outcast he, bewildered and depressed:
> Along his infant veins are interfused
> The gravitation and the filial bond
> Of nature that connect him with the world.
> Is there a flower, to which he points with hand
> Too weak to gather it, already love
> Drawn from love's purest earthly fount for him
> Hath beautified that flower; already shades
> Of pity cast from inward tenderness
> Do fall around him upon aught that bears
> Unsightly marks of violence or harm.

We speak of our mother tongue, and I suppose English is mine, as it isn't my own mother's. At school, she had to memorize another Wordsworth poem, "I Wander'd Lonely as a

Cloud"—about daffodils, even though, brought up in Sri Lanka, she'd no idea what a daffodil was. In this passage, the child not only is too "weak to gather" the flower but also doesn't know the word for it, which may be why Wordsworth isn't botanically specific. The love for the flower flows from the child's love and the mother's and is prior to the organization of the world into categories.

Wordsworth shifts from considering this fusion of mother-love and nature-love an invincible panacea, to weighing its efficacy against eviler powers. Growing up, I came to ask: Why did my parents love me so intensely, always trying to build me up—what exactly was it they felt I must be given the emotional weaponry to overcome? What terrible thirst was that great love-reservoir designed—like one of the enormous artificial "tanks" created by the ancient kings of Sri Lanka—to supply? "No outcast he, bewildered and depressed": their over-love was a preemptive strike, an inoculation against alienation. It's the curse of the immigrant child to come dangerously quickly to the point of knowing, or feeling that they know, more about the world than their parents do. To begin to resent one's parents who can no longer parent, who must instead be tactfully ignored; for whose vanished authority alternatives must be found.

Wordsworth anticipates what we've learned from child psychology, that our first years shape our personality, in particular our ability to be kind to others and ourselves—that "inward tenderness" which might renovate the world. Now that I'm a parent myself, elsewhere (determined to shield Frank from the competitiveness of US school-culture: the AP classes, extracurriculars, the narrativization of one's trauma-overcoming rise to the top), I feel kindlier toward my parents. They knew the dictionary and the other books on the shelves could provide me with, besides an academic boost, something else they could not. It is that idea, of books as a cure for the world's inertia and gracelessness, now as firmly installed in me as the bones of my spine. I can pick holes in the claims we make, sometimes grandiosely, for the value of reading and writing, but a basic faith in books never leaves me. When I open my mouth what comes out is rarely poetry. But it's often *about* poetry, a way of trying to stay close to what feels like verbal magic.

# *Tsunami*

Since we moved to the US, news websites have pummeled me with both British and American crises. The aftermath of Brexit, climate change, the Conservative Party's unending screw-ups, protests following the police murder of George Floyd, QAnon and the invasion of the Capitol, coronavirus variants, the Supreme Court's reversal of *Roe v. Wade*. The bad news never ends, and both the UK and the US are routinely evoked as uniquely awful places perpetually on the verge of crisis: the US news does a special line in "brink of civil war" op-eds.

But I'm also a Sri Lankan, who despairs of this Anglo-American focus and the relentless hyperbole which, in a sense, leaves no language for events elsewhere (or appropriates them at once, as with the carnage in Gaza, to our own culture wars). So it was remarkable to find Sri Lanka, given the scope and gravity of its economic crisis—the worst since Independence—pressure its way onto UK and US news platforms; and, with the storming of the president's residence by a coalition of Buddhist, Hindu, and Muslim protestors (brought together in opposition to a corrupt government), become—briefly—front-page news. Suddenly, newspapers filled with photographs of people resembling me. Protestors usurped the president's luxury swimming pool, his plush suites, his gym. Peacefully (though the police fired water cannons, tear gas, beat journalists to a pulp), they returned millions of rupees found secreted in cubby holes, and turned the mansion into a soup kitchen and a library. This was Occupy Temple Trees: one of the most remarkable events of the twenty-first century, a genuinely radical uprising.

The power of such images inheres in their replacement, of the touristic snapshots of the war-unspoiled South, with which the Sri Lankan government markets its country overseas. In Jaffna in January 2023, water cannons were turned again on Tamil protestors: they pulled out bottles of shampoo and began washing their hair. Again, this counternarrative made some headway into the British and US news, before being superseded.

—

I HAVE WRITTEN several failed novels, some about Sri Lanka (they suffer that burden, of wanting to open the Western reader's eyes), others not. In particular, I seem compelled, over and over, to transplant into fiction my parents' small, cluttered house in the north of England ("not many doctors live around here," remarked a schoolfriend snootily—I've never forgotten). There always comes a point when I digress from the story I'm trying and failing to tell, to describe my childhood home yet again.

Ours is the age of memoir and (mostly, it would seem, for

white people) autofiction. If news in the UK and the US is often parochial, staying close to home, telling us about ourselves and not global others, this self-focus tallies with other anxieties. We worry about the very possibility, let alone the acceptability, of imagining ourselves into other people's lives, as novelists have since the nineteenth century. Another way of looking at this—putting morality aside: how hard it seems, for many of us, to escape the face in the mirror! We seem, feel, mired in personal particularities and peculiarities. Perhaps previous generations actually *could* get outside their own heads, but we no longer can. We have become too present to ourselves. And yet that solipsism is also a matter of enduring, almost unbearable uncertainty. For while young authors are encouraged to "write what you know," the reason I keep trying to describe the house my parents live in and where I grew up is surely because what should be a place of safety and security has in fact always been mysterious to me. I am compelled to write about it in an effort to *get* to know it, and the unspoken intricacies of my own life, better. I yearn to, getting to grips with that haunted house, absent myself of its guilts through bequeathing them to others: characters in novels living lives different from mine. But I can't let go. My fingers clench automatically, around the handful of pebbles I had hastened to throw into the sea.

My parents never throw anything away. The same unused inhaler has sat in the fridge for twenty years. (Why the fridge?) The tooth-whitening strips I brought home from the Midwest still reside in the bathroom cabinet, along with a packet of condoms that expired four years ago. Carved masks hang lopsidedly along the corridor to the dining room, where my mother sits eternally in state, eating her curry and rice—her fingers pinching and kneading more than is necessary, moving small heaps to and fro like chess pieces. Rubbish (cardboard, plastic) is jammed above the light panels in the kitchen, and around the outdated flatscreen there proliferates an endless clutter of knickknacks from Laksala and Las Vegas and Blackpool and who knows where else. This is where my parents spend their lives, watching television, waiting to hear from my sister's family or mine (beneath the glass of the coffee table my father has arranged photographs of the whole family). Only when I visit can they be coaxed to sit in the back garden, in the lichen-spotted deck chairs by the apple tree overloaded with fruit; where the heads of rotted peonies are so heavy, in the summer months, that they bend, even break, their stalks. There we discuss old times, my mother and father complaining in imperfectly learned idioms about the barbecue fumes and rock wafting over the fence from their Sikh neighbor's house.

The cul-de-sac is lit at one corner by a streetlamp tilting in the small patch of grass my father considers ours, and mows—the pillar wants to fall, is levering up a divot of earth by its frail grass strings. It is nighttime. I stand, now, in the dark at the bottom of the drive, home for the holidays from university, having returned tipsily from the pub; pausing, to peel papery strips from the bark of the silver birch. My presence activates the security light (unconnected to any alarm) installed above the garage, beside the comma of rust where my basketball hoop once lived—a *pottu* on the house's brow. Pebble-dash, half-drawn blinds, the ongoing flicker of the television downstairs. Something holds me back. Then I climb toward the front door—that golden light behind the imitation stained-glass roses.

—

WILLIAM EMPSON BEGAN WRITING as a precocious undergraduate a book of literary criticism called *Seven Types of Ambiguity*—published when he was twenty-four, following his expulsion from Cambridge (condoms were found in his room). To read his analyses is like watching a magician pull rabbits from a hat—with a showman's flourishes. But he also shows poems to be like the sites delicately excavated by archaeologists, to reveal besides strata of soil and rock the residues of successive civilizations—one vanished culture stacked on top of another. Empson taught at Peking University, became interested in Buddhism, and his poems stress the necessity of our living with ambiguities rather than denying them:

LET IT GO

It is this deep blankness is the real thing strange.
The more things happen to you the more you can't
Tell or remember even what they were.

The contradictions cover such a range.
The talk would talk and go so far aslant.
You don't want madhouse and the whole
thing there.

Every line in the first stanza rhymes with its equivalent—first, second, and third—in the second (Empson would have rhymed "were" and "there"). He musses the syntax to pinpoint life's inherent oddity. At the same time, these elegantly deformed sentences appear to have broken through surface appearances, mere "talk," to a deeper truth. The literary critic is sometimes expansive and exploratory; elsewhere he (Empson) can be brilliantly, even acidly, summative. Everything narrows to a single point of assertion. When this occurs in the poem, however, we are to take such instants of concentration as themselves mental phenomena that come and go.

—

A PLACE, A HOUSE, gone mad. Where so much has happened, that narration of the past becomes impossible; it might even, if you tried, drive you crazy.

Are my parents hoarders? Is it because of all they lost "back home"—their coconut estate, money in the bank, priceless jewelery, friends and family, status—that they won't chuck, now and in England, anything in the bin? Or have they only ever considered their house in Leeds another transitional space, something with which to make do—a suitcase lived out of, not a property to lovingly perfect nor an investment to maintain? Something strange happens whenever I return, and one or both (they leap in to correct each other) speaks of life in Sri Lanka. Once we've exhausted the standard, tired repertoire of anecdotes that immigrants carry around with them like a battered suitcase of possessions, to inflict on their kin and any stranger crossing their path, it's possible something wholly new to me, a fragment of a past I am only slowly piecing together with each year that passes, may resurface with a swoop leaving the listener—me—grasping for handholds before toppling into the void. An apple falls from the tree; my mother lights a new incense stick, slanting in its holder and emitting a slow curl of ash from the end. She begins to speak. This house, with excruciatingly familiar junk, its everpresent curry smell, makes a new kind of sense. I listen intently, trying not to forget.

—

AS A CHILD, my father traveled to India every year on the ferry; his grandparents lived in Salem, Tamil Nadu. You caught the train to Galoya, eventually attached (the shunting might last four hours) to the Colombo-Mannar service. The packet steamer took another two hours. As it pulled away from the shore, he looked back at the land he was leaving—seeing how distance darkened the green vegetation. Then he ran to the front, outstaring the blank bright sea, seeking India . . .

—

"BRITISH SHIPPING COMPANIES," writes Vivek Bald—of those South Asians who, in the early twentieth century, escaped this exploitative profession, into the US—

> justified their exploitation of Indian workers with a racial mythology that portrayed men from the colonies as inferior to Europeans. Indian men were "weaker," "less capable" sailors . . . more "suited" to the heat of the boiler room (because they were accustomed to a "tropical" climate) or to servile and domestic tasks above deck. These ideas were reinforced by the attitudes of white British

> seamen. Although firing and stoking a ship's furnaces and monitoring, regulating, and maintaining the steam in its boilers required a combination of strength, stamina, and skill, this work was derided by British sailors as . . . fit only for lesser workers.

—

THE ARSON of the Jaffna library in 1981 destroyed thousands of ancient, irreplaceable Tamil documents. I've visited the rebuilt library, and scanned the yellowed clippings and laminated info-sheets pinned in the lobby to the green baize of a glass-fronted noticeboard that, when we arrived at sunset, appeared to bend and melt at its reddish, molten edges like a Dalí clock. Old men sat with big, rumpled newspapers ruffled by the fan overhead. A gummy, homely smell. I wandered the aisles, emerged—unenlightened. Whatever the experience should have been, I'd missed it.

So, in Leeds, I ask my parents. What can they tell me. *It was terrible. Sinhalese thugs. The government was involved. It was genocide*, adds my father—always wanting to put in the last, correct, polysyllabic, English, word.

Then silence. I realize a story is forthcoming. And in that moment, I understand why all my attempts at writing a novel have failed. Why it is, that I fail so wholly at the telling of stories, even jokes.

Even giving lectures, I can only think aloud in bursts, overheard, of digression. Fundamentally—this becomes clear, as my mother begins to speak, with, despite her hawings and malapropisms, an enviable momentum—my parents haven't only kept from me, as their private, unbequeathable, property, the Tamil language; they have also protected me and my sister by claiming forever as their birthright and burden the very idea of historical time. *They* are the storytellers; which makes me forever a listener, reader, a recipient to be held in astonished suspense; capable, yes, of analysis, but never to hold court myself (as my mother did even as a teenager at Jaffna Ladies College, relaying to her peers, while they sat eating mangoes messily, the storylines of films she'd seen during the holidays). To tell stories—my parents seem to say—is to inhabit a realm of intractable frustration and pain and delay, which it is the storyteller's gift to convert, for the listener, into manageable pleasures.

But sometimes the stories my parents tell are more like the storm, that came on us up-country (I was ten or so) with my uncle, killing the electricity and causing the palm trees to flail wildly, and the swimming pool to flood across its pavilion of red tile into the gray, churning sea—and vice versa. My fear infected my mother. She forgot she had lived through countless such events. We raced into my uncle's room. He sat in his armchair, shirt unbuttoned, grinning—the patio door thrown open—wind and spray whipping around the room, the odor of salt and ozone, and chlorine from the pool, overpowering: white flakes of paint were ripped continuously from the wall and stuck in his silver chest hair.

When the stories my parents tell reach this pitch, the events they describe don't feel contained, there's no barrier between them and me. I have to swim those waters of anecdote—carried too far out by the tide, and forever seeking the shore.

—

"AT THE END of the First World War," writes Bald, "dockside settlements of working-class Indian, African, Arab, and other Asian men numbered in the hundreds and, in larger ports like Cardiff and London, in the thousands. Indian seamen sailing into Britain, however, found a less welcoming and hospitable environment. When thousands of white British seamen returned from their war service and sought to reenter the maritime trade, British port cities experienced a wave of riots aimed at driving out 'coloured seamen.' Afterward, the British government launched a series of its own efforts, as historian Laura Tabili puts it, 'to uproot Black residents from Britain by persuasion or compulsion.' "

—

THE FIRST THING my father saw—nearing India by boat—was a curving line of sand. . . .

Compared to my mother's helter-skeltering excursions into memoir, his tales are fussily precise: compromised, even, by what Ted Hughes dismissively called "the literary process." Is my father out to share his past with me (to, even, provide his son, the writer, with something usable) or trying to remember better for his own sake? "My task," wrote Joseph Conrad, "which I am trying to achieve is, by the power of the written word to make you hear, to make you feel—it is, before all, to make you *see*." But Empson's point—it feels like a conclusion, though it's the start of his poem ("It is this deep blankness is the real thing strange")—

survives Conrad's alternative commitment to resurrection, realism, detail. If both past and present often seem as shadowy and insubstantial to us as our imaginings of the future, how to survive—and thrive?

Conrad also wrote—one of his characters said it—that to be born is to fall "into a dream like a man who falls into the sea. If he tries to climb out into the air as inexperienced people endeavour to do, he drowns. . . . The way is to the destructive element submit yourself, and with the exertions of your hands and feet in the water make the deep, deep sea keep you up."

—

SAND. ARID AND PLANTLESS. Off the steamer they chivvied everyone, into a large shed of galvanized iron. The customs officials tore into your luggage, confiscating even a packet of cheese. Then another train: chockablock; dozens hanging from the sides for want of a seat. Everyone shouting and marching up and down looking for a place and trampling on luggage. A sudden lovely reek: *sambar satham*—rice and gravy folded in banana leaves tied with banana fiber. Yoghurt, *murruku*, *vadai*, shells on which—before the train reached its destination—the vendor would engrave your name. Necklaces of cowrie shells.

—

"IT IS THIS DEEP BLANKNESS is the real thing strange." Empson's first line leaps out of the experience (or anti-experience) it describes—still rumpled. The words are in the wrong order, the bed hasn't been made. The weirdness must be jotted down before it disappears. It is in the nature of this hurried and harried glimpse into life's impossible machinery, to—before you know it—be washed away without a trace, like letters a stick makes in the sand before the tide comes in.

But the poem is the trace.

—

LET MY MOTHER BUTT IN—as she so often does. So these stories contend. Not multiple interpretations of the same event, but different events, lives, jostling for attention—announcing themselves . . .

*The palm leaf manuscripts*, my mother is saying. The previous generation all wrote on palm leaves. *All those things are gone. They were not beautiful books and poems like the things destroyed with the library. But even my father's things are gone.* He was an Ayurvedic physician and wrote on leaves the recipes for his medications, incising the letters with an iron stylus.

Tamil has round, flowing letters, so the leaves didn't tear: her father would, to avoid damaging them, skip the diacritics, so the words looked funny and my mother read them out loud laughing at the nonsense they'd become—sat with her cheek leaned against my grandfather's arm. There was the faint odor of his perspiration, the sweetness of the oil rubbed through his hair: he was in the habit of running his hand through his still surprisingly thick, black, glossy hair. The air passing noisily through his mouth and nose as he concentrated. Finally, he wiped the leaf with a pigment darkening the letters—into their swooping, millimetric reservoirs the ink swam and settled.

It was my mother's responsibility, when the leaves were dry, to gather them with string into big bunches and store them in the *pooja* alcove.

—

NOW FOR A STORY of my own. Let me at least try.

—

OUR DRIVER'S FACE was different at breakfast. Determined—intransigent. "He is saying we are going to see today what the tsunami did to the island. We are going to see everything."

Ananthan drove through sand and rubble. The devastation crept up on us gradually, out of the area's normative disorder. Houses in states of incompletion gave way to ruins: passing buildings reduced in a blow to brick husks, we paused at the memorial of luminous stone listing the dead. Between the trees (a new breakwater) the gusty, glowing sea appeared—with the watched mournfulness of a naughty child, tearful, petulant, looking on as a parent or teacher sees to the one they've hurt.

Saddest were the houses tendentiously rebuilt—where an attempt was made to patch things up or recreate from scratch an unconvincing impression of the water-crushed original. They looked timid, ephemeral, with their fences of dried palm leaves mixed with wire and tilted stakes, and panels of corrugated iron stuck in (these were also used for roofing). Between these ramshackle edifices persisted bare, bruised voids where real homes used to be. Sometimes all that remained of the family that lived there was the deep-buried well—an absurd little concrete mouth lifted out of the ground at an angle, like a nail levered up with pliers, and with the brickwork rudely exposed.

Ananthan explained this zone was a Tiger stronghold; he pulled over suddenly, and leapt from the van. We were afraid—with no idea what was going on—then the door opened automatically (slowly, with its familiar noise oddly like the trumpeting of an elephant) and a dry, spiky plant was thrust into my face.

"He wants you to know of this plant. It propagates by rolling on the ground. It is called *Ravana's moustache*."

Now Ananthan talked and talked a wildly rivering Tamil, with my father trying desperately to keep up, to translate for me. "He says an old woman who fasted to death on behalf of Tamils is buried here. The Tigers built a home for the aged in her honor but the tsunami took it all. Yes, yes, I'm telling him . . . He says people don't want to come back here to live because they can hear the ghosts of the dead crying for help. Ananthan says—it's poetic, really—*the tsunami is gone, but its footsteps remain*."

Every shy, modest attempt to reclaim this land was chaos-pervaded. What was the point of rebuilding a wall beyond a moat of smashed half-buried brick, with tangles of barbed wire irremediably blown into crazy, useless shapes? Weed-networks—ivy-resembling, but along the ground, like wires—stretched over humps of sallow sand. White seabirds stood aloofly between bleached leaves. A house was reduced to its bare crux—where walls met—a jagged cross. A roofless building was streaked with black, as when the flame burns down to the wick of a candle and soot bleeds down its side.

Two pillars, isolated in the scrub; squares of brick, raised only marginally out of the dirt.

The place was exceptional even to Ananthan, but his sense of what was appropriate surprised me (he took selfies). A giant leaf from the short, broad palm trees growing here was laid down to warn truck-drivers of deepening sand. The dried needles of casuarinas, dotted with acornlike seeds, carpeted the ground. We walked to the water past three jagged stones where someone had made a fire and discovered a wicker tent with red bedrolls inside for fishermen. Treasure-hunting, I discovered a dead jellyfish, and two chunky, white—marble?—posts from a smashed balustrade, the ends black, as if burnt.

—

VISITING INDIA, my father's family stayed one night with their friend Hakim, who wore his trousers at nipple-height and was a big noise in All-India radio. The next day they took a horse-drawn cart to the bus station: the driver's whip was a stick with a string tied to it. Like a second, golden whip, the tea-vendor in his hut of coconut thatch tossed the liquid in an arc between brass tumblers—to cool it, supposedly, though it always burned your mouth.

Entering Gurusamipalayam, where my grandfather was born, meant surviving the gaze of the guardian gods, sculpted twenty feet high—bulbous-eyed, sword-wielding—before you reached the Murugan temple and, beside it, the Paavadi, where the weavers did their business. It was like a football (soccer) pitch, but with four-foot-high granite pillars in rows, linked by the thread used in the looms. Trees softened the heat. Everywhere small groups of men stood in confab. No women. This is where marriages were arranged.

The family house was small, with built-in cupboards containing silk and gold and colored thread. My great-uncle sat cross-legged before the lidded desk where money was kept. Above the low bench where customers waited to purchase cloth, a long, irregular tidemark was streaked along the wall by the oil in their hair. My great-grandmother's English became confused as her mind deteriorated: *Don't rouse, don't rouse*, she cried, meaning "row," as in argue. After she died, the hand looms were motorized. The sound penetrated the storeroom where my father slept, or tried to. He was terrified of his grandfather, who was obsessed with *rasavatham*—the possibility of making gold from base metals. He sheltered fakirs and sages in the house, hoping to learn from them the secrets of alchemy. Years ago, the family down the street—all of them—committed group-suicide, out of sheer poverty.

—

A TEMPLE IN BATTICALOA, where my father was born, was knocked awry, aslant, by the tsunami. It has been rebuilt, with its tower of protective concrete gods now facing the ocean—to hold the waters in check and prevent a repeat of 2004, when over a dozen countries had their coastlines destroyed and a quarter of a million people were killed. But this old, slanted tower, its paint scourged away, was left as a memorial. In Hambantota, *only* the temple remained standing: people (my mother) proclaimed a miracle, but it was the only building made of concrete; no wonder houses and market shacks were washed away. Near Galle, a man who'd lived through a tsunami in Chile saw the sea withdrawing, recognized what was happening, and led his fellow villagers to high ground—only one died. Passengers on a train out of Colombo weren't so lucky: it derailed, killing over a thousand.

I imagine a scene from a Hollywood disaster film, with vast computer-generated waves curling terrifically like Hokusai's, miraculously arrested—by the temple's tower of gods—just as the water rises to touch feverish streaks in the clouds. Or would the gods simply prevent the storm from occurring in the first place, so no one suspected the world of being built, daily, on prevented terrors?

—

> The contradictions cover such a range.
> The talk would talk and go so far aslant.
> You don't want madhouse and the whole
> thing there.

Empson's second stanza, by rhyming with the first, gives what was a pure, confused exclamation a shape (aspiring to the concrete meaning it doesn't fully achieve). I am reminded of the new temple built not to replace but in addition to the tsunami-slanted original. Empson wrote a book about Buddha statues—their curiously asymmetrical smiles—and I wonder what he'd make of me applying his poem to a Hindu *kovil*, with its hundreds of gods staring out from its exterior like passengers clinging to the sides of a packed Sri Lankan train. His last line sounds patrician: a levelly advice-giving, stiff-upper-lipped English voice warns us off full descent into "madhouse." "Aslant" is an unusual word, of the kind a poet might happen across and save for later use because it is load-bearing (and immediately legible) as well as distinctively shaped. I suspect Empson borrowed it from one of the great literary depictions of madness, and drowning—Ophelia's death in *Hamlet*:

> There is a willow grows aslant a brook,
> That shows his hoar leaves in the glassy stream;
> There with fantastic garlands did she come
> Of crow-flowers, nettles, daisies, and long purples
> That liberal shepherds give a grosser name,
> But our cold maids do dead men's fingers call them:
> There, on the pendent boughs her coronet weeds
> Clambering to hang, an envious sliver broke;
> When down her weedy trophies and herself
> Fell in the weeping brook. Her clothes spread wide;
> And, mermaid-like, awhile they bore her up:
> Which time she chanted snatches of old tunes;
> As one incapable of her own distress,
> Or like a creature native and indued
> Unto that element: but long it could not be
> Till that her garments, heavy with their drink,
> Pull'd the poor wretch from her melodious lay
> To muddy death.

You mean, she drowned? asks Laertes impatiently. "Drown'd, drown'd," replies Gertrude. What is the point of her extended description—is it Shakespeare showing off? No: it is as Conrad said—"My task which I am trying to achieve is, by the power of the written word to make you hear, to make you feel—it is, before all, to make you see." Poetry must risk voyeurism in its effort to give dignity and meaning to Ophelia's otherwise meaningless death.

—

"ONE INCAPABLE OF HER OWN DISTRESS." Writing for CNN about Hambantota, Paula Hancocks observes the grimly resilient refusal by the villagers, of the depressive position:

> Residents who had lost everything, who had seen horror beyond imagination, running up to us to offer a face mask to help cope with the unmistakeable stench of death, trying to give us a bottle of water.
>
> One man even apologized we were not seeing his country at its best, begging me to come back when it was all over so I could experience the true beauty and hospitality of the island and its people. He then resumed the search for his brother, sister and parents.

What can we say—considering those temple gods pushed over by the sea, and the rebuilt tower of gods, the houses rebuilt in the same, dangerous place—about those whose living *depends* on the sea, who cannot afford to leave the coast, even if local ruination of protective ecologies, as well as global changes in temperature, have made this life more perilous than ever?

As Empson also said—centering the same word as in his poem—"life involves maintaining oneself between contradictions that can't be solved by analysis."

—

ONE DAY MY PARENTS will disappear from their sitting room and the objects will remain. I won't, arriving at Leeds by train, be greeted as always by my father's anxious, early-arrived figure, standing like a soldier at his post just beyond the arrival and departure screens, staring into the crowd with the same alertness as that boy sailing to India and back, seeing what was strange and wonderful and already erecting within himself a steel, impenetrable barrier to keep it all out.

I will sift through my vanished parents' things, their writing, recipes, diaries, phone books. Then leave through the front door (with the roses), pausing at the bottom of the drive. My sister will be with me. And the stories we will find ourselves—I imagine—now capable of telling, about the past and about our parents (who will no longer interrupt) will help us decide (in England, in the US) what we wish to preserve, what it is right to burn down, or leave behind to be taken by the waters.

# *Love in the Bush years*

"Are you a terrorist?"

It was the second time of asking. We stood to one side of the checkpoint, the official's hand sunk in my belongings. 2003. On the flight from Heathrow to Ohio, I'd ticked boxes to confirm I wasn't a Nazi war criminal, or involved with organized crime: how strange, that Americans asked absurd questions directly, while in England, you had to peer into the blurred play of the muscles around eyes and mouth, decrypt pauses and stammers and lurches into politically incorrect opining, to grasp the suspicions others had of you.

"I don't think so," I said—watching the skin of his forehead wrinkle into a portcullis.

Into the faces of a French couple who knew only fragments of English, officials shouted slowly.

—

I WAS IN LOVE with a woman twice my age with two children, whom I'd met on the internet, through the "random chat" function on ICQ which paired you with a stranger. We'd shared thousands of instant messages, met overseas, but this was my first stay at her house. If it was painful to have to explain all this to the official, I've qualms even about writing it out—being wary of the seizures and overwritings of the lives of others, that memoirists activate just as ruthlessly as novelists, and perhaps in a crueler way. "It seems to me," writes Kath Kenny, "that we demand far too much personal revelation now":

> As if revealing the most awful things will make the writer's voice more honest, more *authentic*. What was once the liberation of personal revelation can too easily become the burden of compulsory disclosure. . . . It seems more interesting—at least more *refreshing*—to look elsewhere. To consider the self in relation to another.

As long, I'd add, as we don't turn "another" into the grisly spectacle demanded. I would foreground that shimmering space *of* relation, rather than the two people involved. I also believe that as the voices of memoir—rather like our online personae—seem to claim the right to generalize, as the reward *for* self-exposure ("See how helpless I am? Well, here's my hot take about the world today . . ."), an unexamined whiteness often comes to the fore.

—

BUT I DO HAVE TO WRITE about this period of my life—there is much to think about: being dark brown in Bush's post-9/11 America; being in love for the first time, a love shaped through writing floated digitally across the ocean and amounting to a vast correspondence. My enlistment, into a misunderstanding now gone global: our collective decision to privilege online intensities over local life. To treat the internet as the real place, where we strive histrionically and supposedly politically, while devaluing—in contrast—our offline milieu.

Perhaps, then, I can write about such things. But obliquely, opaquely—through, again, poetry. Or prose turning into poetry.

—

MY WIFE ENTERED THE ROOM—as I began this chapter, about an old flame—to share a passage from Virginia Woolf's *Mrs. Dalloway*: "Have you ever read a better description of an orgasm?"

> It was a sudden revelation, a tinge like a blush which one tried to check and then, as it spread, one yielded to its expansion, and rushed to the farthest verge and there quivered and felt the world come closer, swollen with some astonishing significance, some pressure of rapture, which split its thin skin and gushed and poured with an extraordinary alleviation over the cracks and sores! Then, for that moment, she had seen an illumination; a match burning in a crocus; an inner meaning almost expressed. But the close withdrew; the hard softened. It was over—the moment.

Woolf's modernist, experimental, onstreaming prose is, in

its tissues and sinews, poetic: suggestive, lyrical, fascinated by what she called "moments of being." But Jenny's surely right, there is a displaced sexuality here, as when saints envision God's light coming at them like a sweetly piercing spear.

"Is it the passage about the lighthouse, and the stroking light?"

I was confused, thinking of another Woolf novel, *To the Lighthouse*:

> She saw the light again. With some irony in her interrogation, for when one woke at all, one's relations changed, she looked at the steady light, the pitiless, the remorseless, which was so much her, yet so little her, which had her at its beck and call (she woke in the night and saw it bent across their bed, stroking the floor), but for all that she thought, watching it with fascination, hypnotized, as if it were stroking with its silver fingers some sealed vessel in her brain whose bursting would flood her with delight, she had known happiness, exquisite happiness, intense happiness, and it silvered the rough waves a little more brightly, as daylight faded, and the blue went out of the sea and it rolled in waves of pure lemon which curved and swelled and broke upon the beach and the ecstasy burst in her eyes and waves of pure delight raced over the floor of her mind and she felt, It is enough! It is enough!

Countlessly, C—as I'll call my American ex-love—and I wrote instant messages, emails, to each other. Sometimes we shared pictures, or video-called, but preferred not to (she was at first still unhappily married, had to be careful). Laboriously we created a space *in language* where feelings and thoughts could be shared: text on a screen made possible alarming, all-at-once intimacies.

One of the things Woolf's poetry-in-prose considers—recalling the nineteenth-century writing she critiqued—is the difference, if and when there is one, between repression and refinement. What happens when physical desire becomes ungrounded and sublimed into language, deferred in both time and place?

It occurs to me now, though I'd have been horrified by the thought at the time, that the meat of the affair was in the long stretches when C and I *couldn't* be together. The relationship was constructed of words in that space of desiring that language could do something delicious with. Of our actual time together, what remains are dwindling details ("the rotten rags of memory," as William Blake would put it) of the sort writers force into connection, to construct realist fiction of the sort Woolf challenged (and memoir). I remember, for instance, a hotel room in Dublin at midnight, lit flickeringly by the muted television, and C speculatively moving my hand, this way and that, over her breast—like a computer mouse. Hours in her backyard drinking round the firepit: bats nuanced the light-polluted space between the pines, while her ten-year-old son made with a branch sparks leap up to outshine the fireflies. The string hammock tied between the carport and a broken-backed tree covered in moss like water-damaged velvet. Seedlings bedded in old Graeter's ice-cream tubs. C's oversized old Donut Friar T-shirt—so shapeless, it could have been my girlish, undeveloped body under there, and my legs in her man-sized pajamas. In the early days, we made a game of it, taking it in turns to lift each other up and carry the other across thresholds.

—

BUT THESE DETAILS seem beside the point. (Speaking of my own past, Conrad's approach doesn't work: How can I make you *see* what evades even my own glance; how to transmit memories that have never felt like secure possessions?) What Woolf said of the Edwardian writer, spending paragraphs describing the construction of a building, its provenance, before condescending to the minds, bodies, dwelling in it, applies: "He is trying to make us imagine for him; he is trying to hypnotise us into the belief that, because he has made a house, there must be a person living there."

—

INTRODUCING HER TRANSLATIONS of Li Shangyin—the late-Tang poet, who lived in China in the ninth century, over a millennium before the novelists that Woolf attacks, like Arnold Bennett, tried their luck—Chloe Garcia Roberts explains:

> Despite the gaping holes in our understanding of the specificities of Li Shangyin's poetry, his writing has maintained an evolving presence for more than a thousand years. His frequent use of carnal imagery (beds, undone hair, inebriation), his inversions of gender (writing sometimes from the male perspective and sometimes from the female), and his frequent subjects of courtiers and sexual affairs have resulted in him being generally labeled as a love poet. And yet he is not a one-dimensional

> romantic, as the cyclicality and inseparability of longing and bitterness, meetings and partings, love and grief are in continual tension throughout his work. Moreover, the span of this emotional narrative, from the first glimmerings of desire to the last agonies of separation, is often twisted, subverting the laws of action and reaction to create a space where resignation can precede desire, or where pleasure and anguish are simultaneous.

Specificities insist on themselves (the ladybirds, or ladybugs, as C called them, upended on the sill; the magnolia whose petals riddled the melted tarmac). They reassure us with patterns of cause and effect. But a relationship defined by cycles of distance and delay, freighted with otherness—lovers different in race, age, employment, duties of care—occurs *in the mind*, unavoidably, even when touch is possible.

When two people in love know throughout that it must one day end—in a concession to the reality principle, against which our tales of romance usually rebel—every event is multitextured. Words launched across a distance become at best ambivalent, sometimes alleviating the pressure and at other times testing boundaries springing into existence only in that moment.

—

FOX NEWS SAID: Watch out for dark-skinned men with shaving cuts; they may have just shaved off, to disguise themselves, an Osama-like beard.

Stared at, gauche, I went to the upstairs bathroom and attacked my face with C's safety razor—moving cautiously from her sleeping side, where between our bodies her clamshell phone lay pulsing. Her second job, for American Nursing Care, meant answering calls in the dead of night.

Hacking angrily at my beard with the inadequate instrument slowly but surely revealed areas of my face whose callow sullen heft I had forgotten: reddened all over and in some places actually streaming blood, here were my cheeks, jaw, my Adam's apple.

I didn't want to look like a terrorist but I also didn't want to look this young: it meant there was no hope for C and me. Her son's friends already asked him, is that your brother; her fifteen-year-old daughter was horrified. "When you're thirty," C said, "I'll be almost fifty." I'll never be thirty, I told her.

The hair-clogged razor under the too-hot tap: black hairs aswim round the plughole. A further wash of tiny black scratches tidemarking the sides of the basin.

We'd passed the midpoint of another two-month stay. Oxford was starting to lose patience with me for studying long distance (there was no precedent for this). I should have worried about such things, but was preoccupied as always by there being fewer days remaining in C's company than had already gone by. I had never before been so sensitive to the passing of time, struggling to learn to consent to its disappearance.

If I think about time, now, all the time, it is because of my time with C—and without her.

—

ONE OF ROBERTS'S MASTERSTROKES, in her edition of Shangyin, is to include not only her own translations but also those of others. One can read three different versions of this poem in particular:

NIGHT RAIN SENT NORTH

You ask the date of my return.
No date is set.
The autumn pools on Ba Mountain
Welling with night rain.

How will that moment ever be: Together,
Trimming a candle at the west window,
And me, recounting
This rainy spell on Ba Mountain?

trans. Chloe Garcia Roberts

NIGHT RAIN, SENT NORTH

You ask when I'll be back but there is no when.
In the hills night rains are flooding autumn pools.
When will we sit and trim the wicks in the west window
and talk about the hills and night and rain?

trans. Lucas Klein

NIGHT RAINS: TO MY WIFE UP NORTH

You ask how long before I come. Still no date is set.
The night rains on Mount Pa swell the autumn pool.
When shall we, side by side, trim a candle at the

West window,
And talk back to the time of the night rains
on Mount Pa?

trans. A. C. Graham

Focusing, to begin with, Roberts's first stanza: changing "well" to a participle, "welling," she stresses the disconnection between the lovers discussing when they'll next meet, and the pools filling with rain.

What does the world have to do with one's own, personally tortured, schedule of loving? If the deepening and overflowing pools are symbolic—of feelings?—this is hardly pushed through. It is only another perception. He, asked when they'll meet next, says, perhaps aloofly, "No date is set," as if it were out of his hands. Or do these lines evoke in shorthand a conversation which does not end with the setting of a date, that peters out, as the talk of long-distance lovers often does, in anger—as if their separation were the other person's fault? Perhaps it is at this moment that one steps aside, looks out of the window, sees or thinks of the pools and rain.

—

OUR FAVORITE FILM—the DVD we rewatched avidly, the story we reapplied to our own lives—was *Nora*, the biopic of James Joyce with a ridiculous tagline: "The World's Sexiest Writer Had Only One Inspiration." We would begin it over and over again on the combination TV/DVD player in the bedroom before C fell asleep half an hour or so in. Sometimes I turned it off, sometimes I clicked to the menu screen, with its daft plaintive music, so I felt less alone in the dark. Certainly I wouldn't watch on, by myself, to the scene C couldn't bear: where Gogarty taunts Joyce about Nora Barnacle's love letter. All these phrases, he says, *she's just copied them out of a book*. When Joyce confronts her, and she insists everyone experiences love, not just writers, C burst, once, into tears.

How small we both felt, compared to the other: how ineffective were our reassurances. We depended on language to maintain our bond yet both felt the sentences we spoke and wrote were inadequate. Where we could express ourselves only in clichés—lovers resummoning ancient, enduring scripts—we each blamed ourselves, not the other, for the disconnections that followed. We arranged and rearranged our sentiments, like translators returning to a poem down the generations, trying out new words—seeking something durable, words entering, to apply Seamus Heaney, "the sense of touch." In this way, people in long-distance relationships all become writers: people experiencing in an unrelieved way a compulsion to get something out of language that it hasn't the power to give.

—

BECAUSE WE EACH KNEW the relationship would eventually end, things happening on the days we lived, temporarily, in the same place, happened unreally, as if aspiring already to the condition of memory. It is that vertigo, of experience experienced as if already passed, past—imagined, even in the moment of emergence, in the alternative costume of a recalled memory—that Shangyin catches with such dexterity. When here and now becomes too intense, those in love step back, and imagine how they'll construe this moment in the years to come. His poem at the simplest level yearns: *When will we be together for good, and able to reminisce about these difficult times?* That this interpretation doesn't exhaust what it says about the irreconcilability of moments, is proved by how not one but three translators have revisited its sentiments a thousand years after its creation.

—

SHOULD THE TV REMOTE FAIL, or if I had to go to the bathroom—it could have been that night when I shaved off my beard—I might rise, and hear C's boxer scrabbling quietly at the bedroom door. Her bladder was weak and by this point she could barely climb the stairs. As her front paws mounted each step a tremor passed through her haunches. Although it was a question of repeating the same move all the way up, she appeared struck by doubt at each sad increment, as if repeatedly reliving the same instance of potential failure. (Shangyin's glittering, multifaceted poems, pushing language to the point of exhaustion, picturing obsessively impossible consummations . . . ) It was impossible not to inscribe a human weariness into her gestures when she finally relaxed herself gingerly to the ground.

I lead her down through the alien house in the dark, past a scatter of paper plates and strewn party poppers. She doesn't pause as usual to lick at the remnants on the plates. There is no ambition, no desire, in her eyes as she raises them to mine. Pushing open the screen door, I watch her wander into the yard and hunch along the grass near the sidewalk.

—

HOW MUCH DO MOMENTS MATTER? For Woolf, they were close to everything; Dante Gabriel Rossetti, labeling the sonnet "a moment's monument," may have continued Shakespeare's myth, that a poem can immortalize its subject, but he was also thinking in a more modern way, about moments becoming currency, the reason for being, of the lyric poet who writes in a short, charged way about experiences that won't come again, that are preserved in language only as snow frailly preserves the hollow of a ghost of the shape of yesterday's footprint. Robert Lowell, father of confessional poetry—writing about himself, his wealthy family, airing dirty laundry—still knew that a poem cannot straightforwardly reproduce experience. "Poetry is not the record of an event: it is an event," he said—which means, poems happen to us as directly as life, that they are a part of the world to which they add something new; but, also, that they cannot unproblematically resurrect other events, moments of the past we would like to revisit and perhaps play out differently. We are, it would seem, compelled to atomize time this way. For as Lowell also tells us, "we are designed for the moment."

—

FOR WOOLF, MOMENTS ARE, if you like, where religion has spilled itself. In the modern world, of facts not values, the meaning of life is experienced in bursts of feeling only tendentiously reconcilable with more prosaic stretches. The women in her novels aren't experiencing alternations of mania and depression (like Robert Lowell, prescribed lithium)—we are to validate their rare, raw glimpses into the heart of reality. For Lowell, this is human perception arriving at its limits. "We are designed for the moment": impulse-driven creatures existing at the meeting-point of a thousand forces impossible to picture. The moment is what we were made to perceive and so it is how we perceive ourselves—through a lens preventing more light, it may be, than it lets through.

—

"YOU ASK WHEN I'LL BE BACK but there is no when." Lucas Klein's translation of Shangyin's poem experiments with ungrammaticality. It pushes literal statement toward a philosophical language, of concepts words strain to touch. Asking the person we love when they'll come again, it would be intensely irritating to be told, *Well, there is no such thing as time. So this question is meaningless.* But Klein's translation takes us in this direction. It can't read naturalistically, vernacularly, as genuinely urgent talk.

When I spoke with Roberts about her translation, she called the poem a temporal Möebius strip, and explained how—challenging norms, to do with the translation of classical Chinese poetry—she'd tried to preserve, not erase, those obliquities of which Li Shangyin (an outsider in his own time) was so fond.

—

THERE WAS SOMETHING slightly desperate, from the start, about that mini-break. As if we knew our relationship was coming to an end. Things felt try-hard. A getaway to a dry county in Kentucky; we had to bring our own, to the guest-house whose owner couldn't seem (though I'm being unkind) to get over the fact of her own non-hostility to a mixed-race, mixed-age couple. Her face kept lighting up as she surprised herself with another burst of generosity.

"I am sorry, though, about the restrooms. I guess they're for couples who are *really* close . . . " We took turns sneaking into the lobby toilet: the en suite in our room had no door, not even a bead curtain. C and I would never become *that* familiar with each other. There was also a Jacuzzi tub that almost worked, a wardrobe with clawed feet, and a metal table sculpture spelling the word *PARIS*, the hole in the *A* heart-shaped and with red wax stains. I could fly across the Channel from England to France, but never with C—that was a distant dream. Nearer to hand—a few minutes down the road—was the famous waterfall in whose spray glimmered a rainbow, a "moon-bow" on the right nights of the year. It seemed a giant lived in a great cave beneath the overhang, that the fumes were from his pipe. In the evening we visited a drive-in movie theater. Two off-white screens faced, seemed to confront, each other across a dirt lot. We tuned our radio to the dialogue. When Jodie Foster first lost her child on the plane, it seemed—on the vast screen, beneath the wheeling constellations—as if anything might happen. But the payoff was dismal. Carefully, C predicted that the Arab passenger accused of being a terrorist would turn out—she was wrong—to be an FBI agent.

—

ALL THREE TRANSLATIONS of Shangyin's poem mention candles. Candles have become essential to romance, to the idea of special, marked-out, sensual time. There is something overearnest about the shadows they throw, the atmospheric suggestiveness it is their task to impart (Sylvia Plath indites those "liars, candles and the moon"). Culturally coded as feminine—women are supposed to light relaxing candles around their foam-heaped bathtubs—they aren't quite secular, but preserve a ritual magic. The flame is both a gem-like object and a process, in it ideas of ephemerality and constancy collide; the rhyme of "fire" with "desire" is by now too obvious (good only for pop songs) but heat, danger, brilliance, and the curious, as Wallace Stevens noticed, "tearing" of the flame at the wick, as if it wants to be off—the persuadability of fire by tiny movements of the air, its caprice and seeming faithlessness . . . (C and I liked best to dip our fingers in the warm, melted wax, so it cooled into thimbles to peel off and arrange along the table: a way at gatherings of avoiding conversation with others, of retreating into a party of two.)

Yet for Shangyin, trimming the candles is an everyday, or everynight, activity. The agony of his poem is in its countenancing of the impossibility, for the trysting lovers, of their ever experiencing normal, unheightened, unselfconscious time together. Because they are hardly ever together, when they are, it is always like a poem. Every anguished detail shines with a flickering, uncertain light. There is a person inside this poem—or two people—wishing for a less interesting, less poetic life. A life of prose, of sitting together, side by side, unanxiously inhabiting the same moment, without separate, uncommunicated thoughts tearing them apart. It is the unachievable dream of an uneventful togetherness.

—

IF A POEM IS AN EVENT, and not the record of an event, what are we to make of translations? We have three revisitings of Shangyin's poem: an already self-conscious moment, uneasily cloned.

We might talk of something, with difficulty, shared: the poet and his three translators have shared something, as have the lovers; this is one of those poems whose challenge to ideas of uniqueness and unrepeatability must be registered, if we're to claim we've read it at all. Romantic love is a cultural fiction (I don't mean the feelings aren't real). Its parameters perpetually shift. Yet if I cannot return to this poem without vertigo, it comes of the now deeply counterintuitive recognition, that experiences do repeat (can be shared), even a thousand years apart, and for very different people. The human range of affects, of love and despair, joy and terror, is not as million-faceted as history. Thoughts and feelings may tally uncannily with other people's lives, including those long forgotten and those yet to be born.

We used to take such things for granted, in a complacent way that assumed the universality of the experiences of a small group of privileged people. But we may have come too far, in assuming that for every identity there exists a special repertoire of otherwise inaccessible experiences.

—

I AM AWARE, of this affair with a woman twice my age, that it means I had two mothers—including a sexual one. (C, ever-conscious of the age gap, educating me, as if preemptively, in the preferences, the aversions, I was supposed to have: alerting me to her gray hairs, the blue veins shining through her skin like live wires floating in milk.) I seem to accumulate mentors. I manifest in my face and gestures and sentences signals of alarm others hasten to assuage. Advice is given, I am perennially the precocious child, the boy, not the man, of color that (some) powerful white people like to mentor.

The danger, as I've discovered, is of failing to act the role smoothly enough: of appearing, suddenly, as threatening as an equal, with my own opinions and ways of doing things. White mentorship drops away—aggressively. I have ceased to be a child who can be patronized and have become a peer to be resented: in the literary world, and much of academia, there is a great resentment of peers. The veneration of prior generations of writers and scholars, the self-mythicizing of oneself as their heir, goes along with the feeling that everyone on the same level as you—at least those you haven't explicitly allied with—must be fraudulent, or an enemy.

And I am not speaking only about white people. Reading Cathy Park Hong's study of Asian American disquiet, *Minor Feelings*, no passage had me nodding and wincing and dog-earing and underlining so readily as when she speaks about

Asians (who want to be the *only* Asian, in a white space) seeing other Asians as targets to eliminate.

—

C AND I are friends on social media. Sometimes we like each other's posts. She suggested meeting up now that I've returned to the States, but it hasn't happened. Our thousands of emails—comprising a sort of digital epistolary novel—are gone, lost with my old Yahoo email account, which I didn't log into for years and got automatically erased. There should be photographs but they too congest the hard drive of a computer scrapped long ago. The cloud didn't yet exist. Our relationship, its echoes and traces, has not survived into a profoundly altered internet, where the very idea of instant messaging has drastically altered; where video-calls, tweets, TikToks, provide a different, less solitary and concentrated, means of relating not to a small group of similarly isolated beings out there somewhere, but to a virtual audience more or less continuously available.

> How will that moment ever be: Together,
> Trimming a candle at the west window,
> And me, recounting
> This rainy spell on Ba Mountain?

Only in Roberts's translation is there just one person—it would seem—speaking at the end of the poem. The lovers are finally and enduringly "together," but only the poet recounts the events of the past. In the other translations, it's a mutual reminiscing. I have often felt, on the brink of writing to C, that I cannot do so because she wouldn't *want* to revisit these events; it would, for her, forcibly resurrect a togetherness that has passed. "Rainy spell" is a lovely touch. Roberts ties this sort of love to durations dismissible as mere stretches or "spells," just as my sister objected to my relationship with a woman twice my age as a mere "phase"—which it was, but only in the sense that our lives, more discontinuous than we pretend, are always and only a series of overlapping phases, to the point of it seeming (maybe it's night, it's raining, you're looking out of the window by candlelight) that a continuous self doesn't exist, that we are different people at different points in our life.

There is also a feat of contrast in this version of the poem, as the pedestrian "recounting" of the past comes up against "this rainy spell": the magic of the moment, the bewitchment of sheerly heightened experience committing lovers to a present moment that cannot retrospectively, reflectively, be recovered, except in accents of unfulfilled yearning. C and I are with different people now: we have, as they say, our own lives to live. I ended the relationship. I tried to go back on this shortly after. I recounted to her our times together. She said I couldn't convince her, even with this sort of magic.

# *Aerial roots*

Traveling near Trinco, where my mother grew up, I came across a banyan tree in a small village. I've never been one for trees and flowers—being ignorant of their names, and envious of those who can write in a smooth, untroubled way about nature, without culture crashing the party. But banyans are different. And that tree in particular.

At its center, where a shrine once lodged, only rot or char or a mixture could be seen: the trunk, they said, was deliberately destroyed during the war, like many Hindu sites. In a sense, the *original* tree had gone. But the absence at its core provided a new focus: not a mutilated void, but—if I squinted; and as I mentioned, regarding those failed green card photos, I am always squinting—a hearth. A banked fire that could once again leap with light.

Banyans have aerial roots—a possible metaphor, for those of us who belong nowhere, but for that reason can be enkindled in the most unexpected ways by unforeseen conduits of benignity and expressiveness. The roots grow down from the branches and, gradually, into the earth: tentative tryouts (little wooden wires, wavering in the wind, seeming to taste their environment, like the tendrils of a jellyfish) eventually finding their way and becoming as immense as stone columns. It is the holy tree of Hindu myth with its roots in the air. The archetype of all temples: an ecology in its own right, a living creature advancing in several directions at once.

—

REMEMBERING KEATS, and the flowery band we are wreathing every day to connect with the earth—reprieved for the moment by the banyan's shade, from what felt like gold bars of heat crashing down mercilessly from the fire-white sky—I had a vision of its branch-roots continuing both left and right for thousands of years, until, impossibly (the ocean!) they formed a new equator, a tree-ring girdling the whole planet.

The Martinican poet and essayist Édouard Glissant disdained talk of genetic roots—the idealization of the one place each of us supposedly belongs—because it means keeping others out. Teaching epic poetry, I once wondered where to begin with the Western classics: Homer, Vergil, John Milton's *Paradise Lost*—until Glissant showed me the way. Although epics were written thousands of years ago to give nations a sense of collective identity (Vergil did for the Romans what Homer did for the Greeks), we should nevertheless, he says, notice narratives shaped by the opposite: homelessness and migrancy. To diagram a nation and its borders has repeatedly proved impossible, without imagining the ventures of those either struggling homeward (like Odysseus) or—as refugees—seeking a new place to live (like

Vergil's Aeneas). It is impossible to summon the logic of the *root*, says Glissant, without invoking its opposite. That exile he labels *errantry*, playing on the word "error," which originally meant, to go astray:

> The great founding books of communities, the Old Testament, the *Iliad*, the *Odyssey*, the *Chansons de Geste*, the Islandic [*sic*] *Sagas*, the *Aeneid*, or the African epics, were all books about exile and often about errantry. This epic literature is amazingly prophetic. It tells of the community, but, through relating the community's apparent failure or in any case its being surpassed, it tells of errantry as a temptation (the desire to go against the root) and, frequently, actually experienced. Within the collective books concerning the sacred and the notion of history lies the germ of the exact opposite of what they so loudly proclaim. When the very idea of territory becomes relative, nuances appear in the legitimacy of territorial possession. These are books about the birth of collective consciousness, but they also introduce the unrest and suspense that allow the individual to discover himself there, whenever he himself becomes the issue. The Greek victory in the *Iliad* depends on trickery; Ulysses returns from his Odyssey and is recognized only by his dog; the Old Testament David bears the stain of adultery and murder; the *Chanson de Roland* is the chronicle of a defeat; the characters in the *Sagas* are branded by an unstemmable fate, and so forth. These books are the beginning of something entirely different from massive, dogmatic, and totalitarian certainty (despite the religious uses to which they will be put). These are books of errantry, going beyond the

> pursuits and triumphs of rootedness required by the evolution of history.

The logic of the root is pernicious. Wanting to know once and for all who we are, we become brutally streamlined. We put ourselves and others in boxes. Seeking an impossible purity, we purge ourselves of that myriad-mindedness that is our true inheritance, trying futilely to extract from the incorrigible plurality of consciousness the outline of a honed hero on a mission.

We gatekeep, demonize, project, become absolute (intolerant, rigidly yelping): the delicate texture of the individual moment cannot survive our overweening plans to control, conquer, and establish at last a zone of total safety (there is in reality no such place) from which to one-up others or look down on them. As Jahan Ramazani observes,

> One measure of globalization's intensity since the nineteenth century has been, ironically, the counterforce of localization and nationalization, evident not only in the outbreak of a globe-engulfing war but also in stricter requirements for passports, more stringent policing of international borders, and the nation-state's burgeoning power and investments, its greater efforts to shape collective memories and identities. Whether early in the twentieth century or in the twenty-first, revanchist nationalisms can't be understood outside the contexts of the global flows they seek to counteract.

*Blut und Boden*: the Nazi slogan, "blood and soil," tied racial authenticity to one's homeland (requiring the expurgation from it of everyone impure). Since, as Kwame Appiah observes, humans have migrated for eons, "trying to find some primordially authentic culture can be like peeling an onion." It is also to choose—contrary to the existing evidence—to believe that secure coordinates are always possible when it comes to goodness and evil, praise and blame.

—

THE BELIEF THAT WE CAN KEEP these things apart, that purity is possible and, when achieved, will redeem us and ours, while canceling others into a sort of hygienically sealed hell, is perhaps the least interesting of the ideas alive in John Milton's blank verse epic, *Paradise Lost*, written in the seventeenth century to "justify the ways of God to man." How? By authoring the most scandalous fan-fiction conceivable: a retelling of Adam and Eve's departure from Eden.

Book 9 locates the "tree of prohibition," and Eve's plucking of its fruit, as the "root of all our woe." Satan, her serpent tempter, enjoys that "errantry" Glissant wishes to reclaim. Evil associates (for now) with wandering, losing one's way, ending up in the wrong place:

> As when a wand'ring fire,
> Compáct of unctuous vapor which the night
> Condenses and the cold environs round,
> Kindled through agitation to a flame
> Which oft, they say, some evil spirit attends,
> Hovering and blazing with delusive light,
> Misleads th'amazed night-wanderer from his way
> To bogs and mires and oft through pond or pool,

There swallowed up and lost from succor far,
So glistered the dire snake and into fraud
Led Eve our credulous mother to the Tree
Of Prohibition, root of all our woe.

Milton's poem isn't as sure as it pretends, as to where our "woe" really did originate. He suggests "wandering" thoughts and feelings came *before* the plucking of the fruit. We can't pinpoint the exact moment of sin's coming into the world; nor announce, by extension, without doubt who is to blame. Such is the contrary logic of "wandering," that for Glissant uneasily coexists with the logic of the "root."

Wandering is about not knowing exactly where you are, who you are, or whom to take for a friend or an enemy. It is to believe, with Katharine Hepburn in *The Philadelphia Story*, that "the time to make up your mind about people is never." The "root" is about deciding exactly what good is, what evil is, and building a nation-state with a big wall around it to keep miscreants out, and remind those inside of *their* identity: Greek, or Roman. Or British. Or American. In Book 2, Milton claims evil is a real, definable thing, emanating from one particular source, a patient zero who can be contained:

Thus Beëlzebub
Pleaded his devilish counsel, first devised
By Satan and in part proposed. For whence
But from the author of all ill could spring
So deep a malice to confound the race
Of mankind in one root and Earth with Hell
To mingle and involve, done all to spite
The great Creator? . . .

Such is the desire to isolate the "root" of "all ill," in the hope of reversing the contamination which has "mingled and involved" Earth and Hell, good and evil, happiness and unhappiness. This is a purity ethic not so different from the idea that by keeping immigrants out, we can keep dirt and danger beyond our borders: in Book 6 of *Paradise Lost*, we're told that God doesn't mean to "destroy" the rebel angels, "but root them out of Heaven."

—

TRAVELING IN THE NORTH of Sri Lanka, it's common to see people with a leg or an arm missing, a brown stub resembling a big banyan root arrested, suddenly, in time and space—dematerialized. The Tamil Tigers wanted a separate homeland; the Sinhala-Buddhist government, since the cease-fire, has tried to purify the country of Hinduism, replacing temples with stupas. It may seem glib to reduce geopolitics to ideas of self and other, oneness and twoness, but those ideas reoccur throughout history, and for a Sri Lankan shaped by civil war, they feel unavoidable. And so we require alternatives.

—

STUDYING AT OXFORD, I avoided Old English and struggled with Middle English, which felt like an alien language. Chaucer was different: irreverent, skeptical—I got on with him. But the rest was inaccessible: Malory's machismo, the Pearl Poet's religiosity.

In 2021, a miracle occurred. A high-profile action-fantasy

film was made, which, though it wasn't set in South Asia, had a South Asian lead: Dev Patel, playing Gawain, from the anonymously authored fourteenth-century poem where he confronts the forbidding Green Knight. Reading this poem as a student, I was lost. Hunched beneath a green glass lamp in the Bodleian, turning without understanding the pages of that illegibly gnarled poem, my expression must have resembled—to anyone watching—the look on Patel's face when the knight arrives to challenge Arthur and his court. For some reason Gawain puts himself forward. In Simon Armitage's translation:

> I am weakest of your warriors and feeblest of wit;
> loss of my life would be least lamented.

Patel plays Gawain the only way a South Asian *could* play an action-hero in a Western film: gawkily, flashing signals of alarm from his large, perhaps overly expressive, dark eyes. (I haven't yet seen *Monkey Man*, released this year: Patel seems on a mission to change things.) An actual, physical miasma, of disbelief—*Are you sure? Me, the brown bloke? The hero?*—appears to rise in the umbral gloomth of Arthur's meeting-chamber, from his skin absorbing into itself the hue of his unearthly opponent. Turning, that is, brown-green: Pantone 448 C, the aversive shade selected for cigarette packaging the world over (beginning in Australia, in 2012).

South Asians aren't cast as leads in Western cinema or television. Rhik Samadder, who gave up acting and became a journalist, writes of, as a child, being reassured by his father about a school play: "*Neverland isn't a place on Earth, so Peter Pan can look like anything . . . You can be anyone you want.*" But this didn't turn out to be true. "I hated every other job I was sent up for, the majority of which were terrorist dramas":

> There were four good parts a year written for Asians. . . . Strategically, I decided to play possum: I would abandon hope for a while, stop trying, but only until Riz Ahmed was too famous to be going up for the same parts as me, at which point I'd swing back into the game. Which I did, only to start losing them to Dev Patel.

When Patel-as-Gawain looks up, startled, at the entry of the Green Knight, he reminds me of the South Asian actor waiting to hear if he has got the part—astonished by the temerity of a casting director choosing him, for some reason, as the lead.

But there is more to be said of Gawain as played by Patel: a slovenly fuckboy, aimless, dissipated (he has a girlfriend, but won't commit), of whom his mother despairs. I have met this person before. For every high-achieving South Asian child placed under that astounding pressure to succeed which transforms them into gems, another crumbles, drops out, gives up. Patel's Gawain's long hair marks him out. Placeless and with no role model, conscious of being different but not in the right way, he is failing, like many young South Asians, to find his place. This isn't simple race-swapping: to me, Patel plays the fourteenth-century knight *as* a twenty-first-century South Asian man, preemptively emasculated, struggling out from under expectations incommensurable with his desires, but whose persisting heft has so displaced him from any sense of what he might *actually* want, that the only alternative to a stiflingly codified, inexpressive excellence seems to be disorder and despair.

It is, then, as shocking for Gawain to be *brown*, in this bare-bones replica of Arthur's court, as it is for the intruder (and his mount) to be "enker grene" of "hwe":

> The guests looked on. They gaped and
> they gawked
> and were mute with amazement: what did it mean
> that human and horse could develop this hue,
> should grow to be grass-green or greener still,
> like green enamel emboldened by bright gold?
> Some stood and stared then stepped a little closer,
> drew near to the knight to know his next move;
> they'd seen some sights, but this was
> something special,
> a miracle or magic, or so they imagined.

In the film, this amazement, manifested by Arthur, Guinevere, and others, seems displaced from its true origin: not the Green Knight, but brown Gawain, whose difference from his peers goes otherwise unremarked. Extraordinarily—a feat of filmmaking, a profound engagement with, but also a subversion of, the original text—racialized difference appears front and center. Brown and green are both *natural* colors; it is as if the Green Knight were all leaves (he carries a sprig of holly), a literal force of nature, making Patel's skin the bark of the tree, or the color of the earth the knight grew out of. They are two halves of the same entity.

Patel's Gawain's amazement at the Green Knight is matched by his amazement at himself, when he accepts the challenge. He can't seem to believe he has stepped up to the mark. And yet this is the man who will not only strike the Green Knight's head from his shoulders when challenged—but also, once that magical horror, still alive, demands Gawain meet him in a year's time, kneel to receive a blow in return:

> Gawain was motionless, never moved a muscle,
> but stood stone-still, or as still as a tree stump
> anchored in the earth by a hundred roots.

—

SIMON ARMITAGE'S TRANSLATION modernizes the original's intensive alliteration:

> Gawayn graythely hit bydes and glent with
> no membre,
> Bot stode stylle as the ston other a stubbe auther
> That ratheled is in roché grounde with rotes
> a hundreth.

Although as a student I airily dismissed such poetry as primitive (because I didn't get it), and merely violent, the alliterative meter allows for multiple interpretations. The repeated gutturals in the first line, and the *st* phonemes in the second—we still speak of "standing stock-still," or "still as a stone"—give us the feel of Gawain's courageous forbearance from reaction. Previously, he flinched instinctively at the fall of the axe-blade. Now it is as if those sounds each stand for a micro-movement that has been suppressed, in favor of a grave immobility; in the final line, those *r* sounds I dread suggest the plurality of the roots binding with rocky soil. What are the equivalent tent-ropes and tethers of will, that have Gawain hold fast? The stone simile is replaced by a tree, because for unliving stone to remain motionless is no achievement: only a creature that can die may prove its worth by resisting the impulse to flee.

—

TREES DON'T MOVE. Or do they? The banyan—from the Hindi *banian*, or trader; merchants set up shop in its shade—is also known as the walking, the many-footed, tree. Putting down new roots, it can (if the older strands, hardening and thickening into living pillars, are discarded, or die) seem less to expand than drift in the earth: an octopus of morphing wood, hovering through steamy forest, or gradually overtaking and imprisoning within its irregular, enormous, net the ruins of a home left, as so often in rural Sri Lanka, half built, or perforated by bullets; or with its roof torn off and windows eerily dematerialized by the tsunami.

—

THERE ARE TWO TREES of importance in Milton's Eden. From the first, Satan convinces Eve to pluck the fruit of the knowledge of good and evil. From the second, Adam and Eve, having eaten and become self-conscious of their nakedness, snatch leaves to cover themselves. Fig leaves, we say usually, but Milton combines, or confuses, the banana tree (with leaves big enough to wear) with the banyan. We can see what he was thinking. The banyan provides shade from the sun; now, its leaves protect Adam and Eve from being too wholly seen. Milton brings together two kinds of "Indians"—people in South Asia, and those indigenous to what would become the US—and Balachandra Rajan has spoken of these extraordinary lines in terms of the poet's "cumulative infernalization of India." India—the foreign—is hellish. An Indian tree reveals how far human beings have fallen.

But that isn't the whole story. As Adam voices his shame at his nakedness, Milton's verse shimmers with worlds of meaning yet to explore:

> O might I here
> In solitude live savage in some glade
> Obscured where highest woods impenetrable
> To star or sunlight spread their umbrage broad
> And brown as evening! Cover me ye pines,
> Ye cedars, with innumerable boughs
> Hide me where I may never see them more!
> But let us now as in bad plight devise
> What best may for the present serve to hide
> The parts of each from other that seem most
> To shame obnoxious and unseemliest seen:
> Some tree whose broad smooth leaves together
> sewed
> And girded on our loins may cover round
> Those middle parts that this newcomer, Shame,
> There sit not and reproach us as unclean.
> So counseled he and both together went
> Into the thickest wood, there soon they chose
> The fig-tree: not that kind for fruit renowned

But such as at this day to Indians known
In Malabar or Deccan spreads her arms
Branching so broad and long that in the ground
The bended twigs take root and daughters grow
About the mother tree, a pillared shade
High overarched and echoing walks between.
There oft the Indian herdsman shunning heat
Shelters in cool and tends his pasturing herds
At loopholes cut through thickest shade. Those
leaves
They gathered broad as Amazonian targe
And with what skill they had together sewed
To gird their waist, vain covering if to hide
Their guilt and dreaded shame. O how unlike
To that first naked glory!

In the epic poems of Homer and Vergil, armor, prior to battle, is ceremonially donned: we are invited to the performance of a man becoming superhuman, godlike, by fastening to his otherwise ephemeral body greaves and breastplate, hiding his vulnerable face beneath a helmet with a tuft of blood-colored feathers, and, finally, taking up sword and shield and spear. Milton parodies this: Adam and Eve armor themselves with leaves. They want to hide from God and to hide their private parts from themselves and each other, where tree-shadows create a space as "brown as evening."

Brownness, darkness, shame.

—

BUT ALSO, A new kind of "root": multiple not singular. A new kind of—as I see it—holy temple architecture, built not of stone but of living wood. Milton's characteristically sinuous syntax may suggest the outgrowth of sin from a single error, but also dramatizes the evolution of new political structures out of the ether of possibility. (Remember Divya Victor's alternatively multiple and myriad-minded syntax, of kith and connection.) Even as Milton argues for the beginning of all our woe in one act of rebellion, the torsions of his verse encode the counterproposal, of a dynamic, ever-shifting, transnational inheritance beyond simple rootedness.

The tree too has "armes," as the poet continues to play with ideas of war, and armor: Vergil begins the *Aeneid* with his intent to sing of man and his weapons—"arma virumque cano." But the banyan doesn't submit to the metaphor of weaponry and armor so much as absorb and transform it. Martial values are overturned. The banyan is female, not male, it is perpetually giving birth to itself; its seeming pillars of wood are as important as the zones of shade they create, those womb-spaces equally part and parcel of the tree. That birdcage of roots becomes a chamber of echoes, a sanctuary where human sounds gather and rebound.

—

GAWAIN REPOSES IN THE CASTLE of Lord Bertilak (really the Green Knight in disguise), whose wife returns the green girdle his mother said would protect him against harm. Should he wear it, the axe-stroke of the Green Knight won't kill him:

the knight who knew of the power knitted in it
would pay a high price to possess it, perhaps.
For the body which is bound within this green belt,
as long as it is buckled robustly about him,
will be safe against anyone who seeks to strike him,
and all the slyness on earth wouldn't see him slain.

In the provocative film adaptation, Lady Bertilak gives Gawain a handjob while teasing him with the acquisition of the girdle—his semen stains the green cloth. It is a joke, in part, about wearing women's underwear: about how masculinity is constructed. The scene also registers the desire, as intense as sexual desire, for invincibility—as experienced by the fraught, out-of-place, brown knight. It is his lack of trust in himself and his environment, his overriding perpetual sense of operating without the right tools or values in a world of stochastic jeopardy, that has him seek protection.

Like Adam and Eve in Milton's poem, Gawain reveals only his own shame, his inadequacy, in hastening to armor himself. He reveals that all armor is really a rush to cover up one's nakedness, that war-values are inseparable from vanities to do with clothing and usually coded as feminine. Invincibility might seem a far-off dream: fantasy and science-fiction stuff. Achilles was dipped in magical water to (almost) achieve it. But there are many ways of making oneself impermeable to challenge—by hiding, for instance, behind a vocabulary used to dominate others; or by becoming an emotional hermit, before anyone gets to reject you; or by preemptively devaluing the world as meaningless, so one's failures don't sting. These are the lies we tell ourselves and others rather than admit to weakness.

—

DEV PATEL'S GAWAIN is vouchsafed—unlike the original version of the hero—a vision of his possible future. Protected by the girdle, he appears to flee the encounter with the Green Knight; returns home; becomes king. He sits on the throne, his long, bony face dispersing cubistically into affectless gradients.

He doesn't belong on that throne.

Enemies attack the castle. Rubble topples. Carefully, he reaches beneath his ceremonial (the king doesn't fight, doesn't risk his life) chain mail. As if tugging at a loose thread—or tearing, desperately, his own intestines out—he pulls the girdle, achingly slowly, from his waist. When it is done, his head falls from his neck, as if he has at that moment received the long-delayed axe-blow, from the Green Knight. It falls, bounces away, along the ground.

—

AS IF GAWAIN'S HEAD HAD, ever since his second meeting with the knight, *always* been severed, and was merely held in place by that girdle (worn, figuratively, as a choker rather than a belt). In the film, Gawain sees this possible future, chooses against it, removes the girdle, braces for the blow—and, different from the poem (where all ends well, but with an undertone of unease), the film comes to a close with the Green Knight saying, "off with your head": will he strike, or let Gawain go?

What is the meaning of this? Gawain, like Eve, has been tempted. She yearned beyond her station; he wanted to be invincible. The Gawain we see in that flash-forward is—Patel's casting is perfect—the high-achieving South Asian I have met so many times, and in the mirror too, where he trumps me with an expression of amused disdain; the undisturbed composure of one who knows he'll remain a step ahead, that I will never catch up with him.

But he isn't really alive. King Gawain, having made himself immortal, is only a sort of zombie, a man who died long ago when he made the decision, with the taking of the girdle, to seal off contingency and inoculate himself against surprises—both bad and good. Patel excels in this short, counterfactual scene as the sleepy-eyed monarch, his head secretly sewn onto his neck like that of Frankenstein's monster. The price he has paid for quasi-immortality is the peculiar, unscratchable itch, one feels, of that illicit girdle, which, it is made clear, he even wears while making love. I imagine he must suppress the urge to pick at it with his fingers, worrying the fabric; I see him there, sitting in state, fussing with it, as I can't help but pluck violently with my fingernail at the skin around my thumb, or my lips. The temptation to tear the thing off! I spoke of his forbearance from response, as the axe descended toward his neck. Now every moment is a muscular struggle to remain still, a countermanding of the impulse to rip off the girdle—what a relief to finally do it, even if it means death! To die brings to an end his monomania. At last he ceases to be the man gripped by one desire, one object, the feeling that if he doesn't keep growing more and more powerful—as the South Asian child is instructed—in every way, even the most basic subsistence, the most minimally satisfying life, will be denied him.

—

THIS ISN'T TRUE: it is a neurotic fear, which means, a self-centered one. To believe the only alternative to excellence is death is to turn the purposiveness of the migrant into a lethal metaphysics. It is better, I think, for the diasporic South Asian to see the person in the mirror as—more so than many—belonging nowhere, and yet, for this reason, as a creature with many, uncountable, ever-growing, aerial roots. Someone, that is, who puts down roots wherever they happen to be, taking that risk with high spirits, humor, and courage.

The banyan doesn't know what's going to happen. It sends down its wires, gauche strands wavering in the slightest breeze. They touch, tap, the soil, fix themselves there, then widen and thicken. This tree might look like a cage. But there's no one, nothing, trapped inside. It is a picture of true, difficult, freedom.

# ACKNOWLEDGMENTS

Jenny, and Frank.

This book is also dedicated to my whole, extended family, in different countries. Holdens and Midgleys as well as Ravinthirans. Thank you. I am especially grateful to my parents, whose love taught me how to love, and has made so much possible.

I would also like to thank my agents at Wylie, Luke Ingram and Jacqueline Ko; Jill Bialosky and Laura Mucha at Norton; Connor Stait and, formerly, Kiera Jamison at Icon; and Rhiannon Gentile, for chasing up permissions.

Michael Schmidt at *PN Review* and Dai George at *Poetry London*, and Jos Betts at the *Cambridge Literary Review* and Phil Smith at BBC Radio 3, and Rachael Allen at *Granta*, commissioned work rewritten as chapters of this book.

The extraordinary novelist Neel Mukherjee and the extraordinary activist Amika George read early drafts and their comments were invaluable.

# BIBLIOGRAPHY AND APPENDIX OF POEMS

Here is the full text of any poems only selectively quoted in this memoir—with the exception of longer works, for which I've provided line references and listed good editions. Every effort has been made to secure permissions.

Divya Victor, from *Kith* (Fence Books, 2014); whole poem (section) quoted on pages 9–12.

Bhanu Kapil, "27. Who is responsible for the suffering of your mother?," from *The Vertical Interrogation of Strangers* (Kelsey Street Press, 2001):

August, 1967. My father returns to Punjab in the shiny black suit from Marks and Spencer.

My mother almost married the son of The Royal Baker of Rajasthan, who baked, daily, pita breads and almond pastries, for the Maharani of Jaipur. But he was wearing white sneakers when he came to visit her. My mother told her father that she couldn't possibly marry someone who couldn't be bothered to polish his shoes.

Then my father arrives, and says: "I'm leaving for Europe in two weeks." My mother says: "But how can I marry a man who wears socks with red and blue stripes?" But her father, who is tired of placing ads in *The Indian Express* (M.A. Brahmin Girl, Lovely and Fair, Seeks Professional Brahmin Boy, A.S.A.P.), says: "But his feet are so white!"

It's true. My father's feet are hairy, but, nonetheless, after five English summers, ensconced in luridly patterned socks, wonderfully pale. When he takes naps, local urchins sneak into the courtyard, lift up the mosquito net, peer and giggle at these mysterious, cream-coloured appendages.

By the end of the summer, my mother is living in a one-room damp-walled walk-up in Hayes, Middlesex, where George Orwell once taught grammar school English, and where a thirteen-year-old skinhead . . . pours milk bottles of urine into the black—the Paki, the Bangladeshi, the Sri Lankan, the Ugandan, the Ethiopian, the Jamaican, and the Gudjrati—letter boxes.

Biswamit Dwibedy, "Open," from *Hubble Gardener* (Spuyten Duyvil, 2018); whole poem quoted on pages 19–20.

Ada Limón, "The Great Blue Heron of Dunbar Road," from *Bright Dead Things* (Milkweed, 2015):

That we might walk out into the woods
together, and afterwards make toast
in our sock feet, still damp from the fern's
wet grasp, the spiky needles stuck to our
legs, that's all I wanted, the dog in the mix,
jam sometimes, but not always. But somehow,
I've stopped praising you. How the valley
when you first see it—the small roads back
to your youth—is so painfully pretty at first,
then, after a month of black coffee, it's just
another place your bullish brain exists, bothered
by itself and how hurtful human life can be.
Isn't that how it is? You wake up some days
full of crow and shine, and then someone
has put engine coolant in the medicine

on another continent and not even crying
helps cure the idea of purposeful poison.
What kind of woman am I? What kind of man?
I'm thinking of the way my stepdad got sober,
how he never told us, just stopped drinking
and sat for a long time in the low folding chair
on the Bermuda grass reading and sometimes
soaking up the sun like he was the story's only
subject. When he drove me to school, we decided
it would be a good day if we saw the blue heron
in the algae-covered pool next to the road,
so that if we didn't see it, I'd be upset. Then,
he began to lie. To tell me he'd seen it when
he hadn't, or to suppose that it had just
taken off when we rounded the corner in
the gray car that somehow still ran, and I
would lie, too, for him. I'd say I saw it.
Heard the whoosh of wings over us.
That's the real truth. What we told each other
to help us through the day: the great blue heron
was there, even when the pond dried up,
or froze over; it was there because it had to be.
Just now, I felt like I wanted to be alone
for a long time, in a folding chair on the lawn
with all my private agonies, but then I saw you
and the way you're hunching over your work
like a puzzle, and I think even if I fail at everything,
I still want to point out the heron like I was taught,
still want to slow the car down to see the thing
that makes it all better, the invisible gift, what
we see when we stare long enough into nothing.

Tom Paulin, "Contemplation (after Hugo)," from *The Road to Inver* (Faber, 2004); whole poem quoted on page 45.
Nikki Giovanni, "Allowables," from *The Collected Poetry of Nikki*

*Giovanni, 1968–1998* (William Morrow, 2007); whole poem quoted on page 47.

John Keats, "When I have fears that I may cease to be"; whole poem quoted on page 50. Versions of this poem, and the passages from *Endymion* (lines 1–13) and *The Fall of Hyperion* (lines 1–11), are those printed in Jack Stillinger's edition of the *Complete Poems* (Belknap Press of Harvard University Press, 1991).

Cheran, "Ask," from *In a Time of Burning*, trans. Lakshmi Holmström (Arc, 2012):

Ask
snakes, how to copulate. The morning,
how to dawn. Trees, the meaning
of patience. Ask sleep-walkers what colour
dreams are. Refugees, how their tears
became their prison cells. Women and Blacks
who must walk the streets of this town
at night, what fear is. Lovers who wear nose-studs
whether lust lasts for only thirty days.
The monsoon, where the fish have all disappeared,
fish which once sang in the still milk-ocean
beneath the bridge, on full-moon nights.
Ask a lost diaspora, what is born
out of the loneliness of language. Ask her, who flung
a living ember of fire upon the ice-cliffs of my life,
about the quintessential loneliness of grief.
Ask her. And her.

Ask
me,
when the last train of the evening has gone
and the railway lines shiver and break in the cold,
what it is to wait with a single wing
and a single flower.

Robert Frost, "The Most of It," from *Collected Poems, Prose and Plays*, ed. Richard Poirier and Mark Richardson (Library of America, 1995):

He thought he kept the universe alone;
For all the voice in answer he could wake
Was but the mocking echo of his own
From some tree-hidden cliff across the lake.
Some morning from the boulder-broken beach
He would cry out on life, that what it wants
Is not its own love back in copy speech,
But counter-love, original response.
And nothing ever came of what he cried
Unless it was the embodiment that crashed
In the cliff's talus on the other side,
And then in the far distant water splashed,
But after a time allowed for it to swim,
Instead of proving human when it neared
And someone else additional to him,
As a great buck it powerfully appeared,
Pushing the crumpled water up ahead,
And landed pouring like a waterfall,
And stumbled through the rocks with horny tread,
And forced the underbrush—and that was all.

Ingrid de Kok, "Small Passing," from *Seasonal Fires: New and Selected Poems* (Seven Stories Press, 2006):

*For a woman whose baby died stillborn, and who was told by a man to stop mourning, "because the trials and horrors suffered daily by black women in this country are more significant than the loss of one white child."*

1
In this country you may not
suffer the death of your stillborn,

remember the last push into shadow and silence,
the useless wires and cords on your stomach,
the nurse's face, the walls, the afterbirth in a basin.
Do not touch your breasts
still full of purpose.
Do not circle the house,
pack, unpack the small clothes.
Do not lie awake at night hearing
the doctor say "It was just as well"
and "You can have another."
In this country you may not
mourn small passings.

See: the newspaper boy in the rain
will sleep tonight in a doorway.
The woman in the busline
may next month be on a train
to a place not her own.
The baby in the backyard now
will be sent to a tired aunt,
grow chubby, then lean,
return a stranger.
Mandela's daughter tried to find her father
through the glass. She thought they'd let her
touch him.

And this woman's hands are so heavy when she dusts
the photographs of other children
they fall to the floor and break.
Clumsy woman, she moves so slowly
as if in a funeral rite.

On the pavements the nannies meet.
These are legal gatherings.
They talk about everything, about home,

while the children play among them,
their skins like litmus, their bonnets clean.

2
Small wrist in the grave.
Baby no one carried live
between houses, among trees.
Child shot running,
stones in his pocket,
boy's swollen stomach
full of hungry air.
Girls carrying babies
not much smaller than themselves.
Erosion. Soil washed down to the sea.

3
I think these mothers dream
headstones of the unborn.
Their mourning rises like a wall
no vine will cling to.
They will not tell you your suffering is white.
They will not say it is just as well.
They will not compete for the ashes of infants.
I think they may say to you:
Come with us to the place of mothers.
We will stroke your flat empty belly,
let you weep with us in the dark,
and arm you with one of our babies
to carry home on your back.

Alfred Tennyson, *In Memoriam A.H.H*, lines 13–20 of poem 54; quoted from *The Major Works*, ed. Adam Roberts (OUP, 2009).

Solmaz Sharif, section from "Personal Effects," in *Look* (Graywolf, 2016):

How could she say
the things she does not
know. A poison

tipped arrow, she told
classmates at recess,
to the neck, hollow whistle

of it launched
from a blowgun
cutting the air between them.

According to most
definitions, I have never
been at war.

According to mine,
most of my life
spent there. Anthrax

in salt and pepper shakers,
patrol car windshields
with crosshairs painted over them,

some badge holding
my father's pocket contents
up to him and asking

where the cash is from.
The war in Iraq, I read,
is over now.

The last wheels gathering
into themselves
as they lift off

the sad tarmac. I say
*begin*. I say *end*
and you are to believe

this is what happens.
I say *chew 40 times*
*before swallowing*, *slime*,

and you go home to mother,
press a dog tag to your temple,
press a gun to that,

the tag flowering
into your skull. Thank God
for all-weather floor mats

and the slope of my personal driveway
and beer cans that change
color to let me know

they are cold enough.
The full-sized cab
smelling of iron and Axe body spray.

In 2003, a man held a fistful
of blood and brains to a PBS camera
and yelled

*is this the freedom*
*they want for us?* It was from his friend's
head. They were marching

as they figured Americans do.
Between them, hardly three horsepower
and still we shot him.

We say the war is over, but still
the woman leans across
the passenger seat

*my son, my son.*
I wasn't there
so I can't know, can I?

Sujata Bhatt, "Nanabhai Bhatt in Prison," from *Collected Poems* (Carcanet, 2013):

At the foot of Takhteshwar hill
there is an L-shaped house
hidden from the road
by five mango trees
planted by Nanabhai Bhatt.

Huge crows swoop over
the L-shaped terrace,
red-beaked green parrots fight over
the mango trees. Some years the monsoons
sweep away too much.
It is 1930, 1936 . . .
It is 1942:
Nanabhai sits writing for a moment
while my grandmother
gives orders to everyone.

The next day, he lands in prison again:
thrown in without a trial
for helping Gandhiji,
for Civil Disobedience.

One semester in college
I spent hours picturing him:
a thin man with large hands,

my grandfather in the middle
of the night, in the middle of writing,
between ideas he pauses to read
from Tennyson, his favourite—

*A hand that can be clasped no more—*
*Behold me, for I cannot sleep,*
*And like a guilty thing I creep*
*At earliest morning to the door.*

What did he make of the northern trees?
The 'old yew', the chestnut . . .
and the strange season of falling leaves
that comes every year—
Did he spend hours trying
To picture it all?

I know that
as a student in Bombay
he saved and saved
and lived on one meal a day for six months
just so he could watch
the visiting English Company
perform Shakespeare . . .

And I spent hours
picturing his years in prison:
Winter 1943;
it is dark in his cell.
He is sixty years old.
I see him
sitting cross-legged on the floor
and I wonder what he knew
by heart, I wonder
which lines gave him the most comfort.

That semester was endless
with a restless Baltimore March
when the tight buds on the forsythia
teased our blood.
And I, impatient to get on
with other writers
had to slow down
to study that same poem.

So much information
swallowed like vitamins
        for finals—

and yet, I paused at every turn
wondering which parts he had loved.

Anne Ranasinghe, "July 1983," from *At What Dark Point* (English Writers' Cooperative of Sri Lanka, 1991); whole poem quoted on pages 84–85.

Zoë Brigley, "Western Union," from *Hand & Skull* (Bloodaxe, 2019); whole poem quoted on page 94.

Philip Larkin, "Ambulances," from *The Complete Poems*, ed. Archie Burnett (Faber, 2014); whole poem quoted on pages 100–101.

Sharon Olds, "The Sign of Saturn," from *The Dead and the Living* (Knopf, 1984):

Sometimes my daughter looks at me with an
amber black look, like my father
about to pass out from disgust, and I remember
she was born under the sign of Saturn,
the father who ate his children. Sometimes
the dark, silent back of her head
reminds me of him unconscious on the couch
every night, his face turned away.

Sometimes I hear her talking to her brother
with that coldness that passed for reason in him,
that anger hardened by will, and when she rages
into her room, and slams the door,
I can see his vast blank back
when he passed out to get away from us
and lay while the bourbon turned, in his brain,
to coal. Sometimes I see that coal
ignite in her eyes. As I talk to her,
trying to persuade her toward the human, her little
clear face tilts as if she can
not hear me, as if she were listening
to the blood in her own ear, instead,
her grandfather's voice.

Ian Hamilton, "Memorial," from *Collected Poems*, ed. Alan Jenkins (Faber, 2013); whole poem quoted on pages 118–19.

Roddy Lumsden, "Autism," from *So Glad I'm Me* (Bloodaxe, 2017); whole poem quoted on pages 125–26.

Robert Burns, "To a Mouse," from *Selected Poems*, ed. Carol McGuirk (Penguin, 1994):

*On Turning her up in her Nest, with the Plough,*
*November 1785.*

Wee, sleeket, cowran, tim'rous beastie,
O, what a panic's in thy breastie!
Thou need na start awa sae hasty,
  Wi' bickerin brattle!
I wad be laith to rin an' chase thee
  Wi' murd'ring pattle!

I'm truly sorry Man's dominion
Has broken Nature's social union,
An' justifies that ill opinion,

Which makes thee startle,
At me, thy poor, earth-born companion,
An' fellow-mortal!

I doubt na, whyles, but thou may thieve;
What then? poor beastie, thou maun live!
A daimen-icker in a thrave
'S a sma' request:
I'll get a blessin wi' the lave,
An' never miss 't!

Thy wee-bit housie, too, in ruin!
It's silly wa's the win's are strewin!
An' naething, now, to big a new ane,
O' foggage green!
An' bleak December's winds ensuin,
Baith snell an' keen!

Thou saw the fields laid bare an' waste,
An' weary Winter comin fast,
An' cozie here, beneath the blast,
Thou thought to dwell,
Till crash! the cruel coulter past
Out thro' thy cell.

That wee-bit heap o' leaves an' stibble
Has cost thee monie a weary nibble!
Now thou's turn'd out, for a' thy trouble,
But house or hald,
To thole the Winter's sleety dribble,
An' cranreuch cauld!

But Mousie, thou art no thy-lane,
In proving foresight may be vain:
The best laid schemes o' Mice an' Men
Gang aft agley,

An' lea'e us nought but grief an' pain,
    For promis'd joy!

Still, thou art blest, compar'd wi' me!
The present only toucheth thee:
But Och! I backward cast my e'e,
    On prospects drear!
An' forward tho' I canna see,
    I guess an' fear!

Louis MacNeice, "Mayfly," from *Collected Poems*, ed. Peter McDonald (Faber, 2007); whole poem quoted on page 137.

Seamus Heaney, "Broagh," from *Opened Ground: Selected Poems 1966–1996* (FSG, 1999):

Riverbank, the long rigs
ending in broad docken
and a canopied pad
down to the ford.

The garden mould
bruised easily, the shower
gathering in your heelmark
was the black *O*

in *Broagh*,
its low tattoo
among the windy boortrees
and rhubarb-blades

ended almost
suddenly, like the last
*gh* the strangers found
difficult to manage.

Ciaran Carson, "Eesti," from *Collected Poems* (The Gallery Press, 2008):

*I wandered homesick-lonely through that Saturday of*
*silent Tallinn*
*When a carillon impinged a thousand raining quavers on*
*my ear, tumbling*

*Dimly from immeasurable heights into imaginary brazen*
*gong-space, trembling*
*Dimpled in their puddled, rain-drop halo-pools,*
*concentrically assembling.*

*I glimpsed the far-off, weeping onion-domes. I was*
*inveigled towards the Church*
*Through an aural labyrinth of streets until I sheltered in*
*its porch.*

*I thumbed the warm brass worn thumb-scoop of the latch.*
*Tock. I entered into bronze*
*Dark, shrines and niches lit by beeswax tapers and the*
*sheen of icons.*

*Their eyes and the holes in their hands were nailed into*
*my gaze, quod erat demonstrandum:*
*Digits poised and pointed towards their hearts. They are*
*beautiful Panjandrums*

*Invoked by murmuring and incense, hymns that father*
*passes on to father,*
*The patina of faces under painted faces. They evoke*
*another*

*Time, where I am going with you, father, to first Mass.*
*We walked*

*The starry frozen pavement, holding hands to stop*
*ourselves from falling. There was no talk,*

*Nor need for it. Our incense-breath was word enough as*
*we approached the Gothic,*
*Shivering in top-coats, on the verge of sliding off the*
*metronomic*

*Azure-gradual dawn, as nave and transept summoned us*
*with beaded, thumbed*
*And fingered whispering. Silk-tasselled missals. Rosaries.*
*Statues stricken dumb*

*Beneath their rustling purple shrouds, as candles wavered*
*in the holy smoke.*
*The mosaic chapel echoed with a clinking, chinking*
*censer-music.*

*This red-letter day would not be written, had I not*
*wandered through the land of Eesti.*
*I asked my father how he thought it went. He said to me*
*in Irish,* Listen: Éist.

William Wordsworth, *The Prelude* (1850), Book 2, lines 234–51; quoted from *The Prelude 1799, 1805, 1850*, ed. Jonathan Wordsworth, M. H. Abrams, and Stephen Gill (Norton, 1979).

William Empson, "Let It Go," from *The Complete Poems*, ed. John Haffenden (Penguin, 2001); whole poem quoted on page 181.

William Shakespeare, *Hamlet*, Act 4, Scene 7, lines 166–83; quoted from *Complete Works*, ed. Ann Thompson, David Scott Kastan, and H. R. Woudhuysen (Arden, 2001).

Li Shangyin, "Night Rain Sent North," from *Li Shangyin*, ed. and trans. Chloe Garcia Roberts (NYRB, 2018); translations quoted in their entirety on pages 205–6.

John Milton, *Paradise Lost*, Book 9, 634–45; Book 2, lines 378–85;

Book 9, lines 108–115; quoted from *Paradise Lost*, ed. Gordon Teskey (Norton, 2020).

*Sir Gawain and the Green Knight*, Book 1, lines 355–56, 232–40; Book 4, lines 2292–94; Book 3, lines 1849–54; quoted from *Sir Gawain and the Green Knight*, trans. Simon Armitage (Norton, 2007).

## TEXT CREDITS

Excerpt from Divya Victor's *Kith* reprinted by permission of Fence Books.

"27. Who is responsible for the suffering of your mother?" by Bhanu Kapil reprinted by permission of Kelsey Street Press.

"Open" by Biswamit Dwibedy reprinted by permission of Spuyten Duyvil.

"The Great Blue Heron of Dunbar Road" by Ada Limón reprinted by permission of Milkweed Editions.

"Contemplation (after Hugo)" by Tom Paulin reprinted by permission of Faber and Faber.

"Allowables" by Nikki Giovanni reprinted by permission of William Morrow.

"Ask" by Cheran, and translated by Lakshmi Holmström, reprinted by permission of Arc Publications.

"The Most of It" by Robert Frost reprinted by permission of the Library of America.

"Small Passing" by Ingrid de Kok reprinted by permission of Seven Stories Press.

Excerpt from Solmaz Sharif's *Look* reprinted by permission of Graywolf Press.

"Nanabhai Bhatt in Prison" by Sujata Bhatt reprinted by permission of Carcanet Press.

"July 1983" by Anne Ranasinghe reprinted by permission of her estate.

"Western Union" by Zoë Brigley reprinted by permission of Bloodaxe Books.

"Ambulances" by Philip Larkin reprinted by permission of Faber and Faber.

"The Sign of Saturn" by Sharon Olds reprinted by permission of Knopf.

"Memorial" by Ian Hamilton reprinted by permission of Faber and Faber.

"Autism" by Roddy Lumsden reprinted by permission of Bloodaxe Books.

"Mayfly" by Louis MacNeice reprinted by permission of Faber and Faber.

"Broagh" by Seamus Heaney reprinted by permission of Faber and Faber and FSG.

"Eesti" by Ciaran Carson reprinted by permission of The Gallery Press.

"Let It Go" by William Empson reprinted by permission of Penguin.

"Night Rain Sent North" by Li Shangyin originally published in English in *Li Shangyin*, translated by Chloe.

Garcia Roberts, *New York Review Books*, July 31, 2018. Copyright © 2018 Chloe Garcia Roberts.

Excerpt from Simon Armitage's translation of *Sir Gawain and the Green Knight* reprinted by permission of Norton.